Linnea,

please meeting
& having you @

Visalia First.

P.S. Mk

Jeremiah
29. 11 - 13

WHAT OTHER LEADERS ARE SAYING ABOUT MIND VIRUSES

"In his latest book, my friend, Mike Robertson addresses the all important area of our thinking in a fresh, clear and practical way. I have always understood that our thinking, above all things, determines our success. I welcome this resource and believe it will make all the difference in the lives of those who embrace its teaching. Read it, make the mental shifts and watch success begin to flow towards your life."

-Andre' Olivier, Senior Pastor,
Rivers Church South Africa

"Mind Viruses are, unfortunately, something that have been going around since the beginning of mankind. Mike Robertson addresses this problem and brings us the solution. Through Mike's positive lifestyle and way of thinking, he gives us solutions to escape the snares of the mind virus. If you change your mindset you change your mood set."

-Dr. Tim Storey, American Life Coach, Author and Speaker and as seen on Oprah, Los Angeles, CA

"Our mindset influences everything we do. How we handle life with its joys and challenges will be determined by our attitude and our belief system. In his new book *Mind Viruses*, Mike Robertson defines several viruses that can plague our minds and details how these maladies can alter our lives. Knowledge is power, and I encourage you to absorb the wisdom in this book then use your knowledge to establish a Godly mindset that is positive, uplifting and successful."

-Dr. Dave Martin, America's #1 Christian Success Coach and author of "Another Shot," Orlando, FL

"This book will uncover the root causes that have been ailing your vision, mission and God-given purpose."

-Benny Perez, Lead Pastor,
The Church Las Vegas, NV

"This book will sort out your thinking out in such a powerful away that you will have no choice but to move closer to God and see His purposes unfold in your life in a greater measure!"

-Mark Ramsey, Lead Pastor,
Citipointe Church, Brisbane, Australia

"This book is brilliant! Pastor Mike Robertson has written an incredible 'how to' manual for understanding how God has made us and becoming successful in life by renewing our mind. By using the example of a virus, he has helped us to grasp the devastation that unhealthy thoughts cause in our lives. This book shows us that our real battlefield is in our minds and that whatever thoughts dominate our minds really do control our lives. We all face the conflict of mind viruses and in this cutting edge book Pastor Mike gives us the insight to discover and overcome them, so we can live the kind of life Jesus came to give us. If you apply the teaching of this book it will revolutionize your life!"

-Dr. Michael Maiden, Sr. Pastor, Church for the Nations, President
Church on the Rock International, Phoenix, AZ

"The devil attacks us primarily by diluting us or polluting us. My friend, Pastor Mike, has produced something in your hand that serves as an efficacious vaccine and powerful antibiotic to rid toxic thinking that contaminates our lives and condemns us to mediocrity. This is just what the doctor ordered! Prepare yourself for a life-changing experience!"

-Dale C. Bronner, Lead Pastor, Word of Faith, Atlanta, GA

"I have often felt that my biggest adversary isn't necessarily the Devil... it's my own mind. Unlike the Devil- my mind is Omnipresent (always with me), Omniscient (always knows what I'm thinking) and when I let it- Omnipotent (always in control). Identifying and eradicating the virus's and 'stinkin thinkin' that we collect throughout the years, is essential to living a victorious life! Pastor Mike's practical (and often humorous) approach to biblical teaching will no doubt help you find the antidote to the 'sickness within' and ultimately the keys to becoming a true overcomer."

-Troy Lewis, Lead Pastor,
Steamboat Christian Center, Steamboat Springs, CO

"Man has been to the moon, tunneled deep into the surface of the Earth, and explored massive chasms in the oceans. For all the places mankind has conquered, there is one area that remains a perpetual struggle to control. You could say it's the final frontier, except it's the first frontier. The place I'm referring to is the human mind, and the power it takes to master your thought life can only come from God's principles and wisdom. In his new book, Mind Viruses: Diagnosing what's Defeating You, Mike D. Robertson guides the reader into a place of revelation and healing that will help you understand and overcome destructive thinking and replace it with God's powerful truths to unlock your full potential."

-Steve Kelly, Senior Pastor,
Wave Church, Virginia Beach, VA

"When the Apostle Paul said in Romans: "I do not understand what I do. For what I want to do I do not do, but what I hate I do," he was expressing Mike Robertson's concept of a "mind virus." We've all experienced it - situations where self-discipline, study, and focus do very little to fight what we really want to do. And that's why this book is so important. If you're someone like me, who in spite of many years as a Christian, a Ph.D. in Theology, and a wonderful, supportive family, still struggles with my fallen humanity, then this is the book for you. Get it. Study it. Use it. It has the answers you've spent years looking for, and could finally help you change what you thought could never be changed."

-Phil Cooke, Filmmaker, Media Consultant, and Author of "One Big Thing: Discovering What You Were Born to Do," Burbank, CA

"In different seasons of our lives each one of us experience battles that rage in our minds. If not dealt with correctly we could fall short of God's master plan for our lives. In this book Pastor Mike diagnoses the MV that each of us face and gives us the antidote so we can live an overcoming life. This book will help each person to live the life God always intended for them."

-Donavan Cassell, Senior Pastor,
Rhema South, Johannesburg, South Africa

"Every age group can benefit from the wisdom in this book. Young adults who lack vision, need motivation, or just feel stuck, can prepare to be propelled into the destiny that God has for them."

-Ryan Leak, Pastor and Author of "The One"
and as seen on Good Morning America, The Today Show,
People Magazine and CNN, Dallas, TX

"In Mind Viruses Mike Robertson shares from a lifetime of experience helping people achieve success by mastering their thought process through the application of biblical truth and practical insight."

-Dr. Kermit Bridges, President,
Southwestern Assemblies of God University, Waxahachie, TX

"Let me recommend this book to you by my good friend, Mike Robertson. Mike delivers thought provoking and life-changing principles to defeat the negative thoughts which invade our mind, cripple our relationships and hinder our success in fulfilling God's will for our lives."

-Rich Guerra, Superintendent for the SoCal
Network Assemblies of God, Irvine, CA

"Mike Robertson is an authentic leader with the maturity to speak to issues of right thinking that empower our destiny in his new book, Mind Viruses. He creatively integrates practical illustrations with his bedrock commitment to biblical truth transforming toxic thought into the full-blown potential of God's purposes in us."

-Dr. Gaylan Claunch, Asst. Supt. for the Assemblies of God, North TX

"In his new book, Mind Viruses, Mike Robertson helps you identify the barriers keeping you from the emotional freedom you know is possible but haven't yet achieved. Practice the principles Mike teaches and learn to doubt your doubts and fight you fears."

-Dr. Alton Garrison, Asst. General Supt.
for the Assemblies of God, Springfield, MO

"The uncommon truths in this book will be a golden connection to your spirit that will link you and empower you to counter attack these viruses that have tried to limit you, define you and keep you from enjoying the best that God has for you! Get ready to be 'vaccinated' and equipped to put up the shield of faith and quench all the fiery darts of the evil one!"

-Danny Robinson, Senior Pastor,
Life Fellowship Church, Kennedale, TX

"Frustrated and stuck by the side of the road as you try to navigate your life? You are holding in your hands a book that will help you get back on track towards fulfilling your dreams! Mike Robertson will help you diagnose your primary thinking patterns. You will learn why you are stuck and how to get going again. He will show you how to transform your prevailing attitudes. As you enroll yourself in the simple process he prescribes, you will love the results as your future unfolds!"

-Iann Schonken, Lead Pastor,
Family Fellowship Church, Oceanside, CA

"Pastor Mike Robertson is a deeply dedicated, highly motivated, and divinely gifted Man of God. He brings to the table a wealth of experience and insight in His latest book "Mind Viruses" which is sure to serve as an effective tool for any believer who is struggling with overcoming patterns of negative thinking."

-Rick Bloom, Lead Pastor,
Pacific Christian Center, Santa Maria, CA

"Starla and I have known Pastor Mike and Karen Robertson for over 30 years. Mike has always had a unique and clever way of communicating great truths. He's done it again. Mind Viruses will set you free. You won't think the same after reading this book."

-Kendall and Starla Bridges, Lead Pastors,
Freedom Life Church, Dallas, TX

"This is an excellent book for anyone who has ever struggled with how our minds seem to "have a mind of their own." Mike Robertson offers some excellent insights into what causes our mind to head off into dangerous waters. Mike offers some easy-to-understand tips for "bringing every thought into captivity." He talks about the "viruses" that can infect us all, but gives us hope with solutions!"

-Dr. Bob Cook, Senior Pastor of Victory Life Church,
Grand Junction, Fruita, CO

"You are in a war for your soul. The battle for your soul begins in the mind. Mike Robertson will help you win this battle by identifying the enemies' strategy to capture your thought life and reveal how you can have the mind of Christ."

-Gregg Headley, Senior Pastor,
Gospel Lighthouse, Dallas, TX

"Mike masters the process of extracting spiritual energy contained in Scripture and presenting it to readers in practical helps. Mind Viruses offers Mike's pastoral heart and skill moving readers to new appreciation of God's wisdom and raw progress in life."

-Jim Hennesy, Lead Pastor,
Trinity Church, Cedar Hills, TX

"Mike makes a clarion call to gird up our minds knowing that one's thoughts determines one's direction and ultimately one's destiny."

-Elwyn Johnston, Senior Pastor,
Bethel Church, Temple, TX

"As spiritual victory or defeat is first experienced in our thought life, this book on healthy mental attitude is also a safeguard against insidious mind viruses that seek to infiltrate our inner life. With my 55 years of missionary and pastoral work in Asia and the USA, I gauge this book as a must-read for pastors and people in the pew."

-Dr. Fred Mendoza, Senior Pastor,
Charisma Life Church, Pomona, CA

"As Apostle Paul said to the Christians in Corinth, 'Satan, who is the god of this world, has blinded the minds of those who don't believe' (2 Corinthians 4:4). Satan's first line of assault is the mind. Pastor Mike Robertson exposes the manner in which Satan attacks the mind and equips you with scriptural insight to overcome him."

-Sam Rijfkogel, Senior Pastor,
Grand Rapids First Church, Grand Rapids, MI

"Brace yourself; your prison doors are getting ready to open! In Mind Viruses, Mike Robertson systematically dismantles the toxic tools that the enemy uses to imprison and destroy your potential. Freedom is waiting for you!"

-Tim Enloe, Enloe Ministries, Springfield, MO

"The biggest battle we face happens in the mind. It's what moves us forward or holds us back. If you lose here, you lose everywhere. Mike Robertson's new book "Mind Viruses" is the resource you need to help you win this battle. It is written in a way that gives you practical, God given principles that set you up to win. I highly recommend you read this book and put it into practice…it will set you up for inevitable success."

-Chris Sonksen, Lead Pastor,
South Hills Church, Corona, CA

"Mind Viruses" by Mike Robertson is salvation for a society of stressed out and anxious ridden people. He has provided a literary resource for those who want to reNew (not spelling error) their thinking to the fullest sense. It is profound as well as practical and readable as well as rigorous. Mike Robertson has the answer to what is troubling your thinking and help you shift your thinking into a higher gear."

-Dr. Ken E. Squires, Jr., Lead Pastor,
Bethel Life Center, Wichita, KS

"Mind Viruses is an insightful, thought-provoking exploration into how the mind impacts our emotional and spiritual well-being. Mike Robertson successfully illustrates the power these mind viruses can have in our lives and how we, as followers of Christ, can overcome them."

-Connie Hagen, M. Ed., L.P.C., Bastrop, TX

"What you think about today, affects how your life will be tomorrow! With his humor and great stories, Mike Robertson has addressed one of the most important subjects that affect whether or not we will be a success in life. I recommend this book to you!"

-Steve Myatt, Senior Pastor,
Vista Assembly of God, Vista, CA

"The mind viruses that Pastor Mike presents in this book and the solution to them are great tools for a healthy mind and spirit. Staying spiritually courageous, mentally strong, and emotionally healthy require the disciplines Pastor Mike gives in this book. His communication techniques, stories, and Scripture passages lead the reader to desire faith in God's word to eradicate the enemy's attack on the mind."

-Joy Headley, Family Pastor,
Gospel Lighthouse, Dallas, TX

"Tired leaders make bad decisions. Pastor Mike's book will help pastors and church leaders learn to break through the negativity that leads to fear and burn out as they seek to be the leaders God has called them to be."

-William Vanderbloemen, Founder and CEO of Vanderbloemen
Search Group, Houston, TX

"No matter where you are in your spiritual journey, Mike Robertson's "Mind Viruses" is a must read. This book is a remarkable combination of Biblical insight, creative metaphor, and practical application that will "plague" you for the rest of your life!"

-Mike Quinn, Lead Pastor of Newbreak Church,
San Diego, CA

"Too many times we get trapped by our own thinking. Mike Robertson confronts many self-defeating behaviors that can hold your life hostage. He inspires you and gives you solutions that will help you achieve all that God has planned for your future. I urge you take the time and read this encouraging book."

-Tom Westerfield, Lead Pastor,
Southcoast Christian Assembly, San Juan Capistrano, CA

"Mike Robertson is a faithful Pastor, gifted communicator, inspiring leader, and is passionate about leading people into their God-given destiny. A good friend of mine for many years, Mike has something to say that people need to hear. Read on!"

-Steven D. Yeary, Lead Pastor,
Family Community Fellowship, Bakersfield, CA

MIKE D. ROBERTSON

MIND
VIRUSES
DIAGNOSING WHAT'S DEFEATING YOU

Foreword by Dr. Sam Chand

Front cover design by Jon Morris, Fort Smith, AR

Edited by William Simon, Pat Springle, Louise Lessel and Joey Berrios

ISBN - 978-1-4951-5377-8

Published by Dream Releaser Publishing, Inc.

DEDICATION

I dedicate this book to my former Executive Assistant, Louise Lessel. Without Louise, this book or any of my other writings would have never been published. Thank you Louise, for your untiring and excellent commitment to the work of God.

– Mike D. Robertson

CONTENTS

CHAPTER 1: LOOKING IN THE MIRROR...17

CHAPTER 2: THOUGHT PATTERNS THAT BREAK GOD'S HEART 31

CHAPTER 3: DIAGNOSING DEFEAT...45

CHAPTER 4: THE FEAR VIRUS..59

CHAPTER 5: THE PRIDE VIRUS 73

CHAPTER 6: THE DESPAIR VIRUS...89

CHAPTER 7: THE SCIENCE OF THE BRAIN 103

CHAPTER 8: RENEWING YOUR MIND...121

CHAPTER 9: YOUR CREATIVE POTENTIAL 137

CHAPTER 10: THE FAUCET OF GRACE 155

USING THIS BOOK IN CLASSES AND GROUPS.......................................169

"FILLING YOUR PRESCRIPTION" ANSWER KEY 173

ABOUT THE AUTHOR..175

RESOURCES...177

NOTES...178

FOREWORD

NO ONE IS IMMUNE. There is no safe place. There is no preemptive antidote. There is no magic potion, no antivirus serum that can protect you from this virus—the Mind Virus.

This virus infects us without us seeing any symptoms or feeling any adverse effects for a long time. They are transmitted to us, mostly by people closest to us like family and friends—seldom through foes. The latter might be protected against by our defense systems, but people we love, trust and respect can infect us without any malicious intent. A comparison with a sibling by a family member, a public putdown by a teacher, a highlighted inadequacy by a friend; these incidents can infect us with terrible viruses. As my friend Mike Robertson informs us, a mind virus can sit in your system awaiting an opportune moment of weakness and highest susceptibility.

Not only do others infect us with a Mind Virus, we do the same with others. It may not be done intentionally or spitefully, but an off-the-cuff remark, a sarcastic rebuttal, or a throwback on when they messed up can invade those whom we would never harm knowingly.

The most important and significant conversations will never come out of your mouth, but that dialog will ricochet in your mind like a bullet in a metal cylinder. "I'll say this, then she'll say this…" "I know they will make fun of me, but…" "I know they're asking me to do this because they feel sorry for me…"

"No one appreciates me and what I do for them." These internal conversations with ourselves, create an environment and atmosphere which fosters quantum growth of the latent virus. Your Mind Virus then starts showing behavioral symptoms that you are not even aware of—but everyone else is. Stinkin' thinkin' and its odor is smelled by all, except you.

Mike Robertson has written an extremely compelling book from some of the most angst filled moments of his life. He has intentionally designed this book to be informational as well as transparent and transformational, leading to a renewal of the mind. Can you avoid Mind Viruses? No. Can you fight it and win? Yes! Go, be a winner and let your winning infect others for a better you and a better them.

— Dr. Sam Chand

Leadership Consultant and Author of "Leadership Pain"

CHAPTER 1

LOOKING IN THE MIRROR

"Lord, we know what we are, but know not what we may be."
— *William Shakespeare, English Playwright, 1564-1616*

MOST PEOPLE HAVE a real love-hate relationship with mirrors. Each day we roll out of bed and stand before the mirror in our bedroom or bathroom. There, staring back at us, are the prying eyes of our reflection. It is an *inspection reflection*. We stand there evaluating the effect of our beauty sleep from the night before.

If you're a teenager then your all around appearance is a high priority. Time and space become warped while standing in front of the mirror. In front of the mirror an hour feels only like a minute elapsed. The truth is you are mesmerized by your appearance. Every physical change in the mirror is dramatic. Puberty and hormones have perks though, flowing hair, stronger muscles, and beautiful skin. Of course, puberty and hormones also have headaches; zits, frizzy hair, and an inability to fit into last year's jeans. Oh, life is tough! Yet, the mirror never lies.

If you're in your 40s then the morning mirror session is simply an effort to hide the growing realities of age. Teeth seem yellower from all that coffee you've been guzzling down. Crow's feet have landed around the eyes. Gravity seems to be playing tricks on your stomach, thighs and buttocks. Still, you love that mirror. It's the doorway for quality time with your favorite person—you. You trust what the mirror shows you.

By the time you hit your 70s, 80s and 90s, the mirror is comedy. You smile. Your nearly-toothless face smiles back. You need laughter in your life. Levity is good for sanity. Yet, if you see a mole on your cheek, a dark spot on the skin, it's hard not to hit the panic button. The fear of disease causes a lot of *uneasiness* in your mind. One thing is for sure: the mirror forces you to see the good, the bad, and the ugly whether you like it or not.

All of this excitement over our physical appearance in an earthly mirror is time we spend without a second thought. Now, let me ask you: if you could see your spiritual appearance, what you look like on the inside, what would be staring back? What would you see right now if you did a spiritual reflection inspection of your mind? Would it be beautiful? Would it be bad? Would it be ugly?

Personally, if I ever saw a truly hideous reflection staring back at me, like a zombie, I'd be scared stiff. Talk about a creepy, dead thing you wouldn't want to see. Television and movie zombies always seem to spring up from a contagious virus. You know the story: someone gets infected over the weekend and by Tuesday morning everyone on the planet has degenerated into walking dead critters with a ravenous appetite to consume the living. Now, as gruesome, mindless, and vicious those made-up zombies may be, there is something here that has a frightfully real connection with our Christian lifestyle. You see, if we are not addressing our toxic thoughts, it's just a matter of time before we discover the zombie in the mirror. When we are not obeying we're straying, and the abundant life gives way to an ugly beast inside of us.

> **WHEN WE ARE NOT OBEYING WE'RE STRAYING.**

What gives birth to a spiritual zombie? Well it begins with something deceptively small, an infectious bug. What I call a *mind virus* or MV.

THE BUG SEASON

The medical field has always fascinated me. I used to live in the San Diego area only minutes away from Tijuana, Mexico. Our neighbor to the south has very relaxed regulations in administering medicine. Basically, you can be your own doctor, and many people take advantage of this opportunity. To be honest, I'm a Mexico kind of guy; I'm very confident in my ability to diagnose and treat my own illnesses. My wife, Karen, shakes her head when I self-prescribe medicine. She used to work in a pharmacy. She has seen people like me before!

In order to expand my medical knowledge, I studied infections, bacteria and viruses. It was the viruses that caught my fascination. I discovered a single virus controlling one human cell is all it takes to create chaos in the human body. A virus is not alive as we normally think of something alive. This may sound creepy, but it exists on the fringe of life and death. Once inside our bodies, they find a host cell, and attach to it. However, the virus may not attach and multiply immediately. A virus may remain suspended in our bodies for a long time waiting for a host cell to come along. When it finally finds the host cell it quickly takes over the cell's ability to replicate. The virus multiplies into more cells. Like rabbits on steroids, viruses produce millions of new cells in seconds!

Human cells are small, bacteria smaller, but viruses are the tiniest of particles; about one-millionth of an inch across! Some viruses are so small they can only be seen with an electron microscope. It is the perfect microscopic usurper; an infectious zombie in the body of what once was healthy living cells.

A virus can lie dormant in the world around us for thousands of years. Animals may pick up the virus and later pass it along to humans. Viruses enter through the nose, mouth or a break in the skin. Some people come into contact with viruses by consuming poorly cooked foods or drinking contaminated water, while others get it through an infected person via promiscuous sexual interaction. Yet the most common method of infection comes through everyday physical use of our hands that come into contact with contaminated surfaces. Later, we use those hands to stroke our brow, touch our chin, rub our eyes, scratch our nose and touch our lips. Studies show that each of us touches our faces an average of sixteen times each waking hour.[1]

LEFT UNATTENDED, THE MIND VIRUSES RENDER ONE'S FAITH ANEMIC.

By now, you're probably checking the cover of the book. You didn't expect a dissertation on flu transmission and how to avoid it! But there's a parallel between the physical world and the spiritual world when it comes to foreign organisms and substances that attempt to destroy what is healthy and alive. Even as a physical virus infects our body's cells, a

1. "Test Your Smart Germs," Margaret Back, cited at www.divinecaroline.com/22175/104656 test-germ-smarts

mind virus infects our thoughts. If left unattended, this virus in the inner man will replicate into destructive attitudes, actions and lifestyles.

VOICES: CARRIERS OF CORRUPTION

Ever heard of Typhoid Mary? She was a carrier of disease (bad bacteria in her case) living in the New York City more than a century ago. She did not suffer directly from the effects of typhoid, but she was a carrier of the disease. She infected dozens of innocent people by her profession as a cook. No one suspected that the nice lady preparing the food was spreading something lethal. In the same way, negative voices are carriers of poisonous, twisted and destructive thought patterns. Some voices come from the outside: family, friends and coworkers; some voices are inside: demonic teasers and temptations. If these initial thoughts remain intact in your mind, the spiritual virus will replicate and carve out cynical comments that run like looped recordings. You might hear internal comments like this in your head:

- You are so wicked. How can you ever serve God?

- You are a failure. Do you really expect anyone to believe in you?

- God has forsaken you. He let your parents die young. What kind of a God is that anyway?

- The people at church are so spiritual, but they never say 'hello' to you. They should be bending over backwards to get to know you. You can do better. There are other churches.

What's amazing about a mind virus is that it may contain some truth. You may have lost someone, been wronged or failed in a test. The poison is cloaked in a layer of partial truth, but the potency of the lie is designed to make you bitter, rebellious and callous. The Scriptural warning is clear: "Make every effort to live in peace with everyone and to be holy; without holiness no one will see the Lord. See to it that no one falls short of the grace of God and that no bitter root grows up to cause trouble and defile many" (Hebrews 12:14-15).

I love talking to people about the power of the mind—especially imagination. The Apostle Paul explained that "God can do anything, you know—far more than you could ever imagine or guess or request in your wildest dreams!" (Ephesians 3:20 *The Message*). When you begin to tap into God's unimaginable creative power, you will find the jet stream of the Christian life. Sadly though, after working with people for quite a few years, I have come to realize that I can't get folks to dream without first dealing with their mind viruses. Negative, toxic thoughts are mild annoyances for some people while others find dealing with them as a matter of life and death. In a nutshell, how we think matters; *it really matters.*

DAILY INTAKE

Like the human body, our spiritual body is nourished by what we consume on a daily basis. What we take in both internally and externally will affect behavior. You're either eating a feast from "God's heavenly bistro and feeling renewed in your life or lowered yourself to dining at the Devil's trough of junk food where the impurities make you anxious, angry and cynical. Over time you will be stronger or weaker depending on the diet of thoughts your mind chooses to digest.

HOW WE THINK MATTERS—IT REALLY MATTERS.

I haven't been a devoted follower of Christ all my life. During my teen years, I took another direction and my mind was brutalized by nagging voices from the past even as I was attempting to wholeheartedly serve God. Early on, I figured out that two voices could influence direction and choices in life: the *balcony voices* that bring one up and the *basement voices* that tear one down. Each day the voices from above (i.e., fellowship, good counsel, nudges from God, angelic encounters) inject hope and faith in Christ Jesus and affirm one's identity and role in His work; each day the voices from below (i.e., negative and cynical comments, self-righteous quips, relational abuses, and demonic nudges) infest one's mind with viruses rooted in fear, pride and despair. Left unattended, the mind viruses render one's faith anemic. Worse yet, you may wake up one day to discover your spiritual pulse is dead and your heart is cold.

Being older now, I realize how the consequences of sin can affect one's life even years after stopping a particular sinful pattern of behavior. Recently, I had an unexpected and unwanted visit from these voices of the past. I was standing on a street corner in a foreign country contemplating what I was going to eat. As I waited for the traffic to go by, I got this most unusual thought that I should try Ecstasy. I have never seen Ecstasy, but it is a drug that became common in the United States in the '80s when *Raves* (all night dance parties where drugs were often used) were popular. From the research I've done, Ecstasy or "E" is one of those drugs that can have damaging effects the first time you use it. It is a powerful stimulant with hallucinogenic effects that releases a mass of serotonin from the brain. One report regarding global drug use estimated that as many as 25 million people have taken Ecstasy at some point in their lives.[2] In the U.S. alone, over 14 million people have taken the drug at some point in their lifetime with about one million people trying it for the first time each year.[3]

When someone takes E, they will begin to experience the effects of the drug within about 15 minutes. Because of the effects that Ecstasy has on the pleasure or reward chemicals in the brain, users experience a sense of euphoria and well-being, a boost in energy along with enhanced sensory perceptions. The effects of this drug usually last from 3-6 hours depending on the dosage and drug purity. However, when the user begins to come down off E, they feel tired and dehydrated. A person's short-term memory will suffer for a period of time, their appetite will disappear for 2-3 days, followed by 3-5 days of depression. Because of the undesirable physical and psychological side effects, many users will just simply take more of the drug, leading the way to becoming full blown addicts. Studies have shown that serotonin levels can be affected for years after use of the drug.[4] This effect can cause long-term depression, and even suicide in some individuals.

I KNEW AT THAT MOMENT: I'M STANDING IN A PATHWAY.

Now I have been following Christ for years, but on the day of this temptation toward taking E, I was being visited by an evil spirit. It was more compelling than a random thought. I knew at that moment that I was standing in the *pathway of sinners*[5]. It should not have been surprising though. Jesus explained this phenomenon:

When an impure spirit comes out of a person, it goes through dry places seeking rest and does not find it. Then it says, "I will return to the house I

2. "MDMA," Wikipedia, October 31, 2014. Accessed October 31, 2014. http://en.wikipedia.org/wiki/MDMA

3. "What Is Ecstasy?" Ecstasy Treatment Resources. 2008. Accessed October 30, 2014. http://www.ecstasy.ws/what-is-e.htm

4. Ibid. "Ecstasy Side Effects."

5. Psalm 1:1 (NKJV)

left." When it arrives, it finds the house unoccupied, swept clean and put in order. Then it goes and takes with it seven other spirits more wicked than itself, and they go in and live there. And the final condition of that person is worse than the first. (Matthew 12:43-45, emphasis in italics).

The devil wants you back on the diet of death. If your mind has been cleansed by God's saving work, the devil will try his best to tear you down by seductively twisting your thoughts.

MIND BONDAGE

Everitt Fjordbak was a friend and a professor of mine. He had an unusual command over evil spirits. They had a saying at the local psychiatric ward in his town: "If we can't get the devil out of these people with medication, we need to send them to Rev. Fjordbak." And they did.

One night as Pastor Fjordbak was preaching, some people brought a man who was obviously possessed by a demon into the church. This wasn't an uncommon event during his services. Pastor Everitt had just stood up to speak when they brought the man through the back doors and down the aisle. The man's hair was a tangled mess and fell down over his face. He struggled with the men escorting him. It was a pathetic sight. One look at him spoke volumes: he had been battling his inner demons for a long time. The dark circles under his eyes were an indication that he had experienced many sleepless nights. The look in

> **IF YOUR MIND HAS BEEN CLEANSED BY GOD'S SAVING WORK, THE DEVIL WILL TRY HIS BEST TO TEAR YOU DOWN.**

his eyes explained that he was severely tormented. Suddenly, he broke free from the men. With a crazed look on his face, he rushed toward Pastor Fjordbak! As he got closer to him, he began to shout in a voice that didn't sound human, "I'll kill you! I'll kill you!"

Pastor Everitt had seen all this before. In his calm and cool manner, he said, "You won't do anything of the sort. I am going to finish this sermon, and then I'll deal with you."

By this time, the ushers in the church had again taken control of the demon-possessed man. It took four of them to pin him to the floor. They kept him pinned down until the pastor came to the end of the service. For a while, the crazed man yelled, cried, and talked. Before long, he lost his voice. He was still trying to talk, but no sound came out of his mouth. When Pastor Everitt had finished his message, he asked the musician to play the old hymn, *There Is Power in the Blood*. The song is theologically rich and speaks to the bondage that can be broken through the Blood of Christ Jesus:

Would you be free from your burden of sin?
There's power in the blood, power in the blood;
Would you o'er evil the victory win?
There's wonderful power in the blood.
There is power, power, wonder-working power,
In the blood of the Lamb;
There is power, power, wonder-working power,
In the precious blood of the Lamb.[6]

As the music continued to play and people sang each verse, building in volume and authority, the demon-possessed man began to whine and solicit the pastor's attention. He could speak again. He called for the pastor. Everitt approached him and asked, "What do you want?"

A voice that didn't belong to him requested, "Rev. Fjordbak (the demon called him by name), could you please change the song you're singing? That song is tormenting me!" Of course, the pastor didn't stop singing the powerful hymn. Moments later, the man was free from the demon that had held him captive for many years!

ALL BASEMENT VOICES DISTORT GOD'S TRUTH AND TRY TO POISON HIS PURPOSES.

The voices in our minds may not be as powerful as the demonic ones in this man's life, but all basement voices distort God's truth and try to poison His purposes. No matter what our basement voices tell us, they are designed to destroy our love for God and our relationship with people. Infecting you with a mind virus is a way for them to rob you of the peace and strength available to you in Christ. When you hear these voices chipping away at your faith and trying to spawn a mind virus in you then make a commitment to take those devils to church. I talk to evil voices that harass me on a weekly basis. I declare, "Devil, you have harassed me all week. Now I am going to harass

6. Lewis Ellis Jones. There Is Power in the Blood. (Mountain Lake Park, Maryland, 1899).

you by taking you to church this weekend!" If voices of pride, fear and doubt have harassed you then I encourage you to take those voices to the feet of Jesus. When demons start reminding you of *your past,* you can remind the demons of *their future.* Jesus is the ruler over everything, including mind viruses that show up in our lives from basement voices.

YOUR PET MIND VIRUS

In a Christian life series titled *Mind Monsters,* the author Kevin Gerald gives a definition that's very similar to the concept of this chapter. Gerald says, "A mind monster is a negative invader of your mind. They have come to take away your joy, peace, contentment, and they are designed to disrupt your relationships."[7]

IF NURTURED, MIND VIRUSES WILL TURN YOU INTO A MONSTER.

Mind viruses are mind monsters. If nurtured, these MVs will turn you into a monster. You may degenerate into a mindless spiritual zombie who is apathetic about your faith. You may degenerate into a rude and crude ogre using your tongue to wound people around you. You may degenerate into a troll that takes a toll on everyone's patience through selfish, prideful actions. Take your pick. If you allow mind viruses a foothold they will steal your life away inch by inch, and day by day.

Have you ever had a moment when you knew you weren't thinking right? Perhaps you suddenly realized that your self-defeating thoughts were killing your dream to return to school and get a degree. Perhaps you came to see that your sour attitude was costing you that promotion at work. Whatever ailed your mind, you finally came to ask yourself: *Hey, what I am doing here? I don't want to hurt people. I want to help them. I want to do what is right.* The courage to evaluate yourself and change your life for the better is an important step toward maturity and wisdom in Christ.

You identify the mind virus like you would a physical flu. You know those all too classic symptoms—stuffy head, watery eyes, all over body aches. There's no denying it when you have a flu bug. It's a similar process in identifying a mind virus. Here are the symptoms: It starts with a

7. "Mind Monsters." CC Resources, 2014. Accessed October 31, 2014. https://resources.championscentre.org/Browse/Pack/11

memory or voice from your past that shakes your confidence and then moves into your bruised ego. Finally it develops into accusatory language toward family and friends that spews out of your mouth with the force of a giant sneeze! Just like the flu bug, everyone is affected and infected by you. When you have it, there's no denying it. Yes, you've contracted a mind virus. If you want to be successful in God's eyes then you have to take a stand against the negative invaders in your mind. You have to stop the disease. Stop the monster thoughts from the outset.

GOOD MORNINGS START WITH GOD

Have you ever gone to bed happy and content, but woke up troubled? I have. Sometimes, the most frightening part of my day is when I pass by the mirror immediately after I get out of bed. The mirror forces me to think about my physical appearance, but it also causes me to think about my spiritual appearance. Monday can be particularly rough because I second-guess what I said at our weekend services. But self-doubt doesn't only happen on Mondays. We all seem to grumble or feel defeated over a Terrible Tuesday, a Weird Wednesday, a Tough Thursday, a Freaky Friday, a Stinky Saturday or a Sleepy Sunday. Mind viruses of fear, pride and discouragement erode our faith and identity in Christ. It's the devil's way to enslave us and make us unproductive in God's Kingdom.

EVERY MORNING, I MAKE A CONSCIOUS DECISION THAT I'M GOING TO GO TO MY DEFAULT MODE— THE TRUTH OF GOD'S WORD.

Every morning, I make a conscious decision that I'm going to go to my default mode—the truth of God's Word. Once my feet hit the ground, I may hear an old, familiar voice telling me how bad life is at work, family and church, but I counter it immediately. I draw upon a Scripture verse to combat it. Here are a few of my favorite *rejoicing vita-minerals* (i.e., vitamins) that are great heavenly injections to fight off hellish infections:

VITAMIN B1 to Trust God

"Yet I will rejoice in the LORD. I will be joyful in God my Savior." (Habakkuk 3:18).

VITAMIN B4 to Begin the Day Rejoicing

"This is the day the LORD has made; let us rejoice and be glad in it!" (Psalm 118:24, NASB).

VITAMIN C to Rejoice Always

"Rejoice in the Lord always. I will say it again: Rejoice!" (Philippians 4:4).

If you don't *take charge of your day from the moment you awake* then you are susceptible to catching a mind virus. I believe each day we are above ground is a gift from God, and that's why it is called "the present." We need to remember that God has an assignment for us each day, but a mind virus attempts to hijack our thoughts to make sure we don't do what God wants us to do. We're supposed to be the light of the world, but the devil wants to smother that light. We can't be passive and merely hope these thoughts will vanish. We have to be bold and take action! We have to remind ourselves that we are agents of God waiting for our daily assignments. Our roles in God's Kingdom are too important for us to get sidetracked by mind viruses.

> **IF YOU DON'T TAKE CHARGE OF YOUR DAY FROM THE MOMENT YOU AWAKE THEN YOU ARE SUSCEPTIBLE TO CATCHING A MIND VIRUS.**

Let me give you an illustration of our role in God's purposes. Imagine you hear a knock on your door. You answer it. Standing in front of you is a woman from an express shipping company holding a package. The driver looks like she's had a rough day: her hair is a disheveled mess, one lens is missing from her sunglasses, she has no make-up on, her uniform shirt is half tucked in, and the pocket is torn. She looks like she was in a bar fight and lost. The sky behind her has rain clouds and the wind is blowing wildly. She hands you a package addressed to you, and in capital letters the return address HEAVEN is written on it.

You have a choice as she extends that package to you. Are you going to be scared off by her appearance? Are you going to question the representative delivering the package? Are you going to slam the door on the deliverer and blow off the delivery as a hoax? Or are you going to accept the package addressed to you? Are you going to take the gift God has sent you? Are you going to open it with eager anticipation? Hopefully it's a no brainer to sign for a gift from God! Be sure that you take the gift. Don't miss out on what God has for you.

In contrast, no matter how pretty and friendly the delivery person may be, you should refuse to sign any delivery from something negative or destructive with the return address HELL written on it. Sadly, the sacred record—*The Holy Bible*—shows that quite too often many people accept and nurture destructive mind viruses. We take the packages from hell only to unwrap some terrible mind viruses. How does the Lord react to a viral outbreak in you? What about a viral outbreak within an entire community of people? You may be surprised.

FURTHER DIAGNOSIS

1. How would you define and describe a mind virus?

2. Why are people not responsible in controlling their thoughts? Are we even aware when our thoughts are a mess?

3. What are some examples of balcony voices in your life? What are some examples of basement voices?

4. What is one passage of Scripture you use to repel and replace the most common mind viruses in your life? Why is that passage powerful to you?

5. As you read this book and apply its principles, what do you hope God does in your life?

FILLING YOUR PRESCRIPTION

1. We are not _____we're _____, and the abundant life gives way to an ugly beast inside of us.

2. A virus can lie _____ in the world around us for thousands of years.

3. If left unattended, this virus in the inner man will replicate into _____ attitudes, actions and lifestyles.

4. What's amazing about a mind virus is that it may contain some _____.

5. I have come to realize that you can't get people to dream without first _____ with their mind viruses.

6. I figured out that two voices could influence direction and choices in life - the _____ voices that bring one up and the _____ voices that tear one down.

7. All basement voices _____ God's truth and try to _____ His purposes.

8. Every morning, I make a _____ decision that I'm going to go to my default mode - the _____ of God's Word.

9. If you don't take charge of your day from the _____ _____ _____, then you are susceptible to catching a mind virus.

10. You should _____ to sign any delivery from something _____or destructive with the return address HELL written on it.

CHAPTER 2

THOUGHT PATTERNS
THAT BREAK GOD'S HEART

"Happiness doesn't depend on any external conditions, it is governed by our mental attitude." — Dale Carnegie, American Motivational Author, 1888-1955

YOU SIT AND WATCH the words FATAL ERROR float innocently across a darkened screen. You scream at the computer monitor, "Arrggghhh!" Congratulations. You've joined the ranks of the frustrated; you are one of millions with a crippled computer operating system. The corruption of the hard drive may involve unwanted data, wiped out records, and non-functioning programs. And imagine, the entire mess began with a tiny, malicious, electronic coding commonly referred to as a virus. How appropriate.

Biological viruses are known for their stealth in infiltration, rapid replication, and capacity to adapt and mutate. Now malicious electronic viruses transmitted by the Internet through electronic ads, email (spam) links, and corrupted USB thumb-drive memory sticks have devastating effects on our computers. These destructive codes erase files, inject foreign data, and reformat and disrupt operating systems. The damage is so severe that it may take days or weeks before you have things up and running again.

The reality of a biological or electronic infection that can paralyze and hurt how we function always hits our panic button. Fortunately, in the realm of computers, we can often limit the damage if we act quickly with the right countermeasures. Even after computer viruses have done their worst, information often can be restored and the computer repaired with a good technician and a good restoration program, but that takes money and time. Prevention, in the end, is the best strategy. Having a good virus protection program can prevent most attacks. Setting your computer up to run regular updates, and personally monitoring what sites you visit gives protection as well.

Mind viruses—corrupt, negative, disbelieving thoughts that multiply and mutate—will cause damage in a person's life as sure as an electronic virus can shut down your computer. In cases where we have entertained these viruses in our minds for too long, the Lord may give us a strong restoration program involving wisdom, accountability, and humility to get us on the right track again. Nothing is lost with the Lord. Of course, the best way to deal with mind viruses is to actively run God's antivirus program (the Scripture) in your operating system (the mind). You can get your daily updates from God through prayer. And even as you go to certified, trusted online sites with a computer, you have the Spirit's discernment to frequent godly sources of information—that is, wise leaders and wholesome events. It's all part of keeping the operating system of your mind in peak performance in Christ Jesus. Is it any wonder that the Apostle Paul says, "We demolish arguments and every pretension that sets itself up against the knowledge of God, and we take captive every thought to make it obedient to Christ" (2 Corinthians 10:5).

For us to recognize a spiritual virus, react to its invasion, and reverse any damage, we need to first look at the biblical record of how God sees these insidious invaders of the mind. How does the Lord send us warning signs that we are playing with something dangerous—micro-monsters of the mind. How does the Lord respond to a MV that has spread among His people—a community of believers?

GOD HEARS AND SEES EVERYTHING

The funny thing about mind viruses is that we think it's a private internal conversation—a dialogue of the bad and the good with our inner man. Just because the person sitting next to you has no idea of the battle raging in your mind, doesn't mean that God doesn't know. He knows, and He cares. The writer in Psalm 139 makes it clear, you can run, drive and fly to the ends of the earth, but the Spirit of God is there. Nothing is hidden from God's sight.

Why is that important to know? Because entertaining a mind virus is not a private affair in the secret parts of your mind. When you give birth to sin, God sees it, hears it, knows it and feels sorrow over it. Your wicked little incident may as well be a rock-and-roll concert in God's Bose sound system of accountability. One of the best examples is a guy who was known to be "a man after Gods own heart." Good ol' King David—the shepherd boy, musician and warrior who loved God. Wow. What credentials…right? Well, David entertained a mind virus that started out small (David thought it was a private thing), but it grew, replicated, took over his personality, and nearly destroyed his life. When David took his eyes off the Lord, he became driven by his selfish ego and wrongfully used his position of authority.

LOUNGING AROUND FOR A MIND VIRUS?

Temptations are tough to resist or flee when you are not where you need to be (wrong environment) and doing what you need to do (flaking on responsibilities). You may have a hard time recognizing a mind virus if you aren't fulfilling God's daily assignment by listening in prayer and cherishing His Word in your heart. That's what happened to David.

David knew when he was a teenager that God would raise him up to be king one day—Samuel the prophet had delivered the news. Years later David became the guy on the royal throne. God's expectation was that David be an honorable servant-king by upholding responsibilities of his office, administering just decisions, and walking humbly in private and public matters. David was good at listening to God on a daily basis. David's mind gravitated to asking, what's my assignment today Lord? He was sensitive to when God nudged him to do honorable and praiseworthy things.

Yet, there was a particular year of David's life where he abused his power as a king. A mind virus had taken root. The replication of sinful thoughts began over a beautiful woman named Bathsheba—the wife of a man named Uriah who served in David's army. David may have stood a chance of resisting the virus if he had been doing what God wanted him to do and if he had been where he was needed. Instead, he made himself vulnerable to a MV infection (i.e., "looking for love in all the wrong places"). Here is what happened:

In the spring, at the time when kings go off to war. David sent Joab out with the king's men and whole Israelite army. They destroyed the Ammonites and besieged Rabbah. But David remained in Jerusalem. One evening David got up from his bed and walked around on the roof of the palace. From the roof he saw a woman bathing. The woman was very beautiful, and David sent someone to find out about her. The man said, "She is Bathsheba, the daughter of Eliam and the wife of Uriah the Hittite."

Then David sent messengers to get her. She came to him, and he slept with her. (Now she was purifying herself from her monthly uncleanness). Then she went back home. The woman conceived and sent word to David, saying, "I am pregnant" (2 Samuel 11:1-5).

Did you catch the beginning of this chapter? The writer gives us a great clue about how a mind virus comes along. We're told that in the spring season (the time "kings go off to war") David was lounging around the palace. David was not fulfilling his obligations as a ruler. He may not have been sinning at that moment, but he was far from being wise. Maybe his mind virus was, "*I deserve a break from the boys. I know that I am supposed to be leading my men, but what's the harm in having a playday in the middle of the work month?*" Or maybe David thought, "*I hired Joab to be a general. I'll let him do the heavy lifting on the siege, and I'll show up for the finalities. It's not essential that I lead.*"

AT FIRST GLANCE, MANY MIND VIRUSES DO NOT APPEAR TO BE A BAD THING.

At first glance, many mind viruses do not appear to be a bad thing. MVs can be coated in a personal agenda that rationalizes vanity and selfishness. Mind viruses distort your identity and God's identity. MVs prioritize your wants to exclude God's nudge and His call in your life. MVs can be very subtle and they can breach the security doors of your mind with no fanfare or alarm. If you tolerate or entertain the MV it will replicate into more sinful thoughts and acts.

The story in 2 Samuel is a disturbing record of events. Why? Because David isn't acting like the David we see in early chapters. The noble leader is now a manipulative, lying, carousing, cruel, selfish and callous man. David's MV of lust quickly replicated into physical action—adultery and murder. You see a cold-hearted David come to the surface when a messenger (sent by Joab) arrives in Jerusalem to give a full report of recent casualties on the battlefield. Take notice to David's response.

The messenger said to David, "The men overpowered us and came out against us in the open, but we drove them back to the entrance to the city gate. Then the archers shot arrows at your servants from the wall, and some of the king's men died. Moreover, your servant Uriah the Hittite is dead."

David told the messenger, "Say this to Joab: Don't let this upset you; the sword devours one as well as another. Press the attack against the city and destroy it. Say this to encourage Joab."

When Uriah's wife heard that her husband was dead, she mourned for him. After the time of mourning was over, David had her brought to his house, and she became his wife and bore him a son. But the thing David had done displeased the LORD" (2 Samuel 11:23-27).

There is one more haunting component to this passage. Look at how the chapter ends. Did you know that God is not mentioned throughout the chapter until you reach the last line? When you entertain a mind virus and give into sinful desire, God is pushed out of the picture of your mind (or so we think). The reality is that the Lord is aware of all of it—who can escape God's Spirit? We become spiritual zombies because we foolishly position ourselves to be where we should not be or to entertain temptations we should not entertain. Our lives are exposed before Him. God knows we are His children. He will patiently and lovingly admonish

> **THERE ARE TIMES GOD WILL TAKE DRASTIC MEASURES TO SAVE YOU FROM YOUR SINFUL SELF.**

and exhort us back to love and good works. There are also times that God will take drastic measures to save you from your sinful self.

Often, God's first response to our sinful failures is to wait and offer us the opportunity to willingly come back to our senses. If we don't, He then sends messengers and messages to turn us back to the light. That's what happens in the next chapter when the prophet Nathan confronts David over the murder of Uriah and sin with Bathsheba. Fortunately, David repents. However, the shepherd-king would have to humbly wrestle with the consequences of his sinful behavior in later years.

One of the most crucial ways to win the battle of the mind is to not allow internal viruses to breakout into sin by placing yourself (your mind) in vulnerable venues where the temptation is magnified as in the case of King David with Bathsheba. Neutralize the tempting aspect of a mind virus by simply fulfilling your duties and obligations as God's servant in your daily assignment, and in your life's role as a father, mother, son, daughter, brother, sister, grandpa, grandma, nephew or niece. Don't be lazy. Like the old folk's quote says, "Idle hands are the devil's workshop." When you aren't doing what God intends for you to do each day or when you are not fulfilling your role as a leader, servant, man, woman, counselor, patient, employer or employee, you are permitting good things to be destroyed, through negligence. It's a bad MV that has taken hold of you.

RECOGNIZE AND NEUTRALIZE VIRUSES EARLY ON

Some MVs haunt us regardless of what we're doing or where we might be, because these MVs attack our insecurities rather than our lusts. The Apostle Paul wrote a letter to one of his young protégés—Timothy—who had struggled with mind viruses all his life. Timothy was young and inexperienced. Paul encouraged Timothy to focus on the internal dialogue raging within. Timothy had to deal with the basement voices fueling mind viruses of fear, inadequacy and failure. Paul knew that these MVs would eventually take over and stop Timothy from going where God wanted to take the young preacher. Listen to Paul's counsel: "For God has not given us a spirit of timidity, but of power and love and discipline" (2 Timothy 1:7, *NASB*).

It's important that in winning the battle of the mind to recognize the messages from God and those that come from the pit of hell. We have to discern the source of all incoming messages affecting our mind. It's not always easy to see the difference because so many dark thoughts sound so reasonable. We need the clarity and wisdom that come from God's truth, God's people and the Holy Spirit.

Paul also encouraged the believers at Ephesus with these words: "and be constantly renewed in the spirit of your mind [having a fresh mental and spiritual attitude]" (Ephesians 4:23, *AMP*). If you want to live a victorious Christian life, you have to fight the battle in your mind at the start of each day. You have to consume God's wisdom, His Word, pray, fellowship and share the Gospel to have your spiritual immunity at peak performance. The mind is where the enemy attacks most often, and that's where we're most vulnerable because we don't think anyone is watching or hearing the internal dialogue raging with us, but God is aware. His truth has power over the forces of darkness. In your mind you must replace the basement voices with balcony voices; fight hellish infections with heavenly injections; adjust the low security firewall setting of your mind to the highest setting; and, stop those annoying pop-ups and ads of the mind that tempt and tease you to do what is sinfully destructive.

MY OWN MIND VIRUS OUTBREAK

The devil loves a viral outbreak of sin in a person, and enjoys it more when it runs rampant through the Church and in the community of the lost. Satan is a bitter spoiler of God's creation who enjoys hurting God by marring His creation and His beloved Church. Jesus clearly articulated the difference between Satan's goals and God's when it comes to our spiritual health and growth. The Lord says, "The thief comes only to steal and kill and destroy; I have come that they may have life, and have it to the full" (John 10:10).

Strained childhood circumstances and relationships can hardwire you to think in particular ways that aren't helpful. If you don't identify and replace those mind viruses early in life, you can carry them into relationships with your wife, kids, in-laws, friends and coworkers. Of course, Satan wants you to be a mind virus carrier, and wants you to have an outbreak of sin from the mind virus at the time you and your loved ones are most vulnerable. The devil is interested in one thing—your self-destruction. Never forget it.

> **THE DEVIL IS INTERESTED IN ONE THING—YOUR SELF-DESTRUCTION.**

I grew up in a large family in West Texas. Others who grew up in big families know the unique challenges and dynamics of having strange conglomerations of people for immediate and extended family members. I had seven brothers and sisters. In this environment, someone is going to have a bad day almost every single day! I rarely remember everyone being happy at the same time. Of course, when we were unhappy, we would try to find someone to blame at home. Growing up without much money or possessions tends to make you fight fiercely over any little thing you own. You are quick to blame the other person when something breaks down or is lost. All of us grew up with a habit of finger-pointing and blaming others.

When I decided to become a follower of Christ, I began working in a coffeehouse ministry. Back in my day, coffeehouses were cool places to hang out—this was long before Starbucks was on every corner. We provided games, music, coffee and other non-alcoholic drinks to get people off the street so we could tell them about Christ. In our coffeehouse, my friend Stan and I decided to enter a foosball tournament. Everything was going fine until we begin to lose. Then it happened: An angry, critical nature raised its ugly head within me! Right in front of the people we were trying to win to Jesus, I began to bark my frustrations at Stan. He didn't appreciate it one bit. He'd had enough of my complaints, condescension and pride. He pulled me aside and growled, "What do you think you're doing? You're making a fool of both of us—and we're trying to show the life of Christ to these people!"

His words struck me to the core. Stan's honesty pinpointed where a mind virus had become entrenched in my thoughts and had distorted my character. For the first time in my life, I realized I had internalized a destructive, negative message—blaming others when things went bad—a grumbling, self-righteous attitude. This perspective had taken root while I was growing up in adverse circumstances, and I had carried it with me into the next phase of my life. Thank God that the spiritual immune system He has given us through the Word, sound fellowship, prayer and sharing the Good News renews us even when we feel inadequate. The Lord builds in us an attitude of humility to advance His Kingdom.

UNEXPECTED MV BREAKOUTS

Imagine driving down the freeway when suddenly (seemingly out of nowhere) a nagging temptation or shameful memory jumps into your mind. You've tried for years to ignore those thoughts, but they won't go away. It gets worse when in despair you think, *I wonder what it would be like to drive my car into the concrete wall. I want to end it all right now.*

Do you think for a moment that God gave you the idea to drive your car into a wall and end your life? No, it's definitely not from Him. Do you think you came up with that on your own? No way. It may seem like it, but there's another source feeding you that destructive idea. You have been victimized by what the Bible calls "a fiery dart" from Satan. Paul described it: "...taking up the shield of faith with which you will be able to quench all the fiery darts of the wicked one" (Ephesians 6:16, *NKJV*).

Consider the source of another horrible thought. Maybe someone has hurt you deeply. You think, *I'd like to scratch her eyeballs out!* Where in the world does a thought like that come from? You've been victimized with a thought bomb from hell, and you have one of two choices. You can continue to dwell on that thought and let your anger boil or you can divert your thinking back to a message from above—a balcony message—involving God's love and sovereignty.

Thoughts are like airplanes, they take you somewhere—and not always where you want or need to go. If you stay focused on the negative path of thought, you've

THOUGHTS ARE LIKE AIRPLANES, THEY TAKE YOU SOMEWHERE.

taken the flight away from joy, love, peace and meaning. Instead, you're on the flight that leads to bitterness, self-pity and blame. I call this destination: Negative Town. Many have lived their whole lives at the wrong thought airport, catching flight after flight that always leads back to the same place and now they've lived so long in Negative Town that they can't imagine any other way of life. It's obvious when a person lives in Negative Town because you need only listen to what comes out of their mouths.

I enjoy traveling, flying to far off destinations or driving down the coast of California. My travels have encouraged me to use airplane and highway images and examples in teaching and personal reflection. One is where I picture myself heading down the Life Freeway and coming to a fork in the road. I can take the exit ramp into Negative Town or I can keep going down the freeway and take the exit to Happyville. As we think and pray, God gives us guidance, but many people are still confused. If we can't connect the dots between our words and our hearts, we won't see the choices we need to make. When we realize our words reveal a heart that's out of touch with God's love, truth, and purposes, we're ready for a change. This isn't a once-and-for-all decision. We have to make dozens or even hundreds of choices each day. We learn to live our lives in continual repentance. We are always turning from basement voices to balcony voices, and living to please God instead of conforming to the world's ways. God wants us to make these choices wherever we may be: in the boardroom or the bedroom, on the road or on the sofa. If we don't come to Him daily, those mind viruses get out of control and spill over into what we say and do. As a result: the outbreak jumps from our mind into the minds of those around us. It's contagious and dangerous.

WIDESPREAD OUTBREAKS

Mind viruses take root in a person first. If permitted, MVs eventually break out into every aspect of that individual's life. Yet, what happens when mind viruses sweep over an entire community of people? Is that possible? Can it happen? Has it happened in the past? Well, yes it can happen. It has happened many times.

Nearly three thousand years ago, a people called the Moabites (neighbors to the east of Israel) worshipped a god called Chemosh. Their kind of worship involved sacrificing their children into the flames of the stone idol. Horrific! Yet, how did they come to such depravity? How did child sacrifice become widely accepted? What made it an acceptable behavior by tens of thousands of people? More than likely some Moabite leader in the past committed the first physical act of child sacrifice and everyone saw it as the popular way to be in favor with the ruler. I bet if we push deeper into the problem, we'd find that it all began with a mind virus. My point is this: One person with a MV replicating sinful, negative, destructive behavior can easily spread poisonous thinking into a larger community.

History is packed with mind viruses breaking out into groups of people. These mind viruses are distortions as to who we are, who God is, and how to treat family, neighbors and coworkers. The Bible has quite a few outbreaks recorded:

- Lot failed to see the growing mind virus of sexual weakness growing in his family by living in Sodom where sexual sins were rampant. The Scripture says, he "pitched his tents near Sodom." Every morning Lot exposed his family to a community that had taken perversion to an entirely new level.

- Joseph's brothers had a mind virus of pride and envy that moved them to sell Joe into slavery.

- Solomon had a mind virus where he loved his wayward wives more than loving God.

- Aaron had a mind virus that led him to craft a golden calf for the rebellious Israelites. Later, the Israelites praised the idol as the god that had freed them from Egyptian slavery.

- The disciples competed with each other for the number one slot with Jesus rather than being servants to one another—MVs of pride surfaced over and over.

Take your pick. In the Bible there's always a person with failures and weaknesses you can find kinship with and understand. We all fall short of God's glory - even in the halls of our local church. MVs can be obvious to all or subtle for many. They can penetrate and take root in places and people that normally should be healthy and safe from such negative, destructive thinking. No matter how MVs pop up, where they come from, or even if you can recognize them at first glance, one thing is for certain: God is always heartbroken over mind viruses taking hold of us.

FURTHER DIAGNOSIS

1. Have you ever found yourself in a group or community of people where their MV outbreak was in conflict with your values in Christ?

2. Have you ever been a MV carrier—someone who spreads a negative thought or attitude to others? How did God help you see you had such a problem in your life?

3. Why does God forgive us for our sins related to mind viruses when we humble ourselves, but leaves us to deal with the consequences to our failure?

4. What are the widespread mind viruses prevalent in our culture today, and what kind of sin is it replicating in public?

5. In your opinion, what is the most powerful mind virus infecting the Church in your city, state and country today?

FILLING YOUR PRESCRIPTION

1. For us to _____ a spiritual virus, we need to first look at the _____ records of how God sees these insidious invaders of the mind.

2. You may have a hard time recognizing a mind virus if you aren't fulfilling God's daily _____.

3. Many mind viruses do not _____ (at first glance) to be a bad thing.

4. God's first response to our sinful failures is to wait and offer us the opportunity to willingly come back to our _____.

5. Paul encouraged Timothy to focus on the internal dialog _____ within.

6. The Devil loves a viral outbreak of _____ in a person, and enjoys it more when it runs rampant through the Church and in the community of the lost.

7. The devil is interested in one thing – your _____ - _____.

8. I can take the exit ramp into _____ _____ or I can keep going down the freeway and take the exit to Happyville.

9. One person with a MV replicating sin can easily _____ poisonous thinking into a larger community.

10. _____ are like airplanes, they take you somewhere.

CHAPTER 3

DIAGNOSING DEFEAT

*"Once you replace negative thoughts with positive ones,
you'll start having positive results."* — Willie Nelson, American Musician

HAVE YOU EVER NOTICED how many popular crime and mystery shows are on television? In the last fifty years TV, has produced countless law enforcement stories about police officers, detectives, FBI and CIA agents, Homeland Security guys, covert operations, and bounty hunters. You name it and there is a program for it. Here's a short list of some favorites: CSI, Castle, 24 Hours, NCIS, Law & Order, Twin Peaks, Dexter, Monk, The Mentalist, Sherlock, Murder She Wrote, Hawaii Five-O, Magnum PI, 21 Jump Street, Columbo and Dragnet. If you did a marathon viewing of these shows, you would see a curious fact surface. Sooner or later the characters end up talking to a coroner or reading the medical examiner's report. Why? It's because the coroner has to be painstakingly thorough in establishing the cause of death.

Pastors are often spiritual coroners—we think a lot about spiritual death and life. Counseling people of all ages, being around different congregations in different communities, and sharing in the struggle of families, pastoring gives one a sharp eye on the human condition. It's amazing how the mind can die under a barrage of negative, corrosive and destructive thoughts. Today, there are a lot of mind viruses going around; there are plenty of spiritual dead people loaded with venomous poison—resentment, hatred, bitterness, arrogance and envy.

For me, I think one of the most destructive mind viruses today is religious thinking. It comes from the family group of MVs rooted in vanity and pride, but there are varieties that come out of other MV families like fear and despair. Religious thinking is stuck with remembering the way things used to be or the way it has always been done. Folks caught up in religious thinking totally miss what is about to happen around them and what God wants to do in them.

BREAKING FENCES IN OUR MINDS

The Pharisees, in the days of Jesus, were masters of religious thinking. They had the Ten Commandments that God had given Moses, but they didn't feel ten rules were enough, so they added 613 more! They called these rules *fences* as they were barriers to keep you from even getting close to the Big Ten. For example, the commandment, "Remember the Sabbath and keep it holy" seems easy enough to follow. The Pharisees, however, decided it needed more rules to further explain what God meant. They burdened the people with added regulations that told you how far you could travel on the Sabbath and how much of a load you could carry. They were building fences of religious thinking while all around them the everyday people were dying in the ditches.

> **TODAY WE HAVE RELIGIOUS THINKING RUNNING RAMPANT.**

Today we have that kind of religious thinking running rampant. We have to guard against this deadly MV. We have to cross those fences in our minds; we have to break loose with the Lord's wisdom, kindness, mercy, compassion and grace. It reminds me of a story about a minister who was driving out of Baton Rouge, and noticed a group of prostitutes on the side of the road. One of the young ladies was obviously very pregnant. It broke his heart, but he knew his ministerial peers wouldn't approve of his stopping or being seen associating with her. He fought the battle in his mind and finally decided to turn his car around and see if he could help her.

When he arrived to where the young lady was standing, he got out of the car and quickly said, "Lady, I have no desire for your body, but I want to help your soul."

Embarrassed by the entire situation she was in, she hung her head and quietly whispered, "I am two weeks past delivery." Then pointing to a car across the street where a man was sitting in a car, she continued, "See that man sitting in the car? He's my husband. We have no food and I need to turn a trick so we can eat today."

The minister was so heartbroken by the woman's plight that he took both her and her husband home with him. The pastor later took them to a church where an evangelist named Dudley Hall was holding a revival. The woman's husband went forward to accept the Lord. The next day, the woman was in labor and her husband had a job. It all started from a right decision where fences had to be crossed. Breaking out to do what God wants done brings freedom, healing and salvation.

NEW THINKING BREAKS FREE

In the second chapter of the Gospel of Mark, Jesus talked about breaking out of old, destructive, negative thinking when His disciples were criticized for not following the old religious way of the Pharisees. Jesus shared and taught that true freedom was found in following Him, and that did not sit well with the regulations-minded Pharisees.

Instead of getting into a long debate with the Pharisees, Jesus used illustrations. He said, "Let me put it this way, fellas: You wouldn't take a brand new piece of cloth and put it on an old garment and then wash it, because the new cloth will rip apart the old cloth, and you don't want to do that." The Pharisees must have had confused looks on their faces because Jesus went right into a second illustration that they were very familiar with—wine-making. Back in those days, everyone drank wine because they didn't have Coca-Cola. Everybody knew about wine-making because that's what they drank with all their meals. So Jesus said, "Guys, you know about making wine. You wouldn't take this year's wine and put it in an old wineskin that is two years old. You all know what that would do." They replied, "Oh yeah, that would explode that old wineskin."

The Pharisees seemed to be grasping the concept a little more so He continued: "So what you need to understand is that I'm bringing something new in, and if you have an old wineskin, you're not going to be able to handle this new thing that I'm doing. I'm asking you to get a new you. I'm asking you to have a *new thought life*. I'm asking you to get rid of the old thinking that is permeating your life, because you cannot go where I am taking you with old thinking."

Let me give you a practical example. Karen and I took our first church outside of Fort Worth, Texas. I remember that first Sunday when we were there. I was getting ready for the Sunday night service, and I walked by one room and heard some voices inside. So I peeked into the room and there were a bunch of men in a classroom having a study on Revelation.

I opened the door and greeted everyone, and they said, "Pastor, come on in here and study the book of Revelation with us." I said, "Fellas, I don't know. I'm heading to get ready for service."

They nodded like they understood. As I was about to leave one of them said, "By the way, Pastor, are you a millennialist, mid-millennialist or post-millennialist?" I was standing there scratching my head trying to figure out who was cussing at me when another man spoke up and asked, "Pastor are you pre-trib, mid-trib or are you post-tribulation?"

At this point, all eyes were on me seeing if I would pass this first test as their new Pastor. I looked around the room and confidently said, "Well, fellas, I'm none of them, I'm a pan-trib." They all looked shocked! Then one brave soul asked, "What's a pan-tribber?" I said, "I believe it's all going to pan out in the end, baby. I'm planning on going up on the first load. But if it doesn't happen like that, it's just seven more years and I believe it's going to pan out in the end."

Do you see how they were hung up in religious thinking? I don't have time to be bothered with religious thinking. People can sit around all day and talk about how many angels can sit on the head of a needle, but I've the Lord's work to do: there are people who need to be born again, people who need healing, and people who need to hear the Good News that God loves them! I don't have time to be bothered with all of this old religious thinking—it only gets one in trouble!

In the late 1990s we were planting churches down in Mexico. I would set up trips where young people could go down to the Baja California area in the summertime to do missionary work. One day, I was driving around with our missionary, David Godwin. We were looking for churches willing to act as hosts for these young people coming to serve in Mexico. One day, we pulled into this one church on a gorgeous piece of property! I thought to myself, *This will be a nice place to put some young people!* We got out of the car. We walked no more than five steps and my missionary friend got back in the car and said, "Let's go. Let's get out of here."

I said, "What? David, this looks like a nice spot. We could put twenty-five young people here. They could win this area for the Lord."

He again said, "Let's get out of here!"

I strolled over to where he sat and leaned on the car. I asked him through the open window, "What's up?"

"Look on the wall," he replied. "You see all those names on the wall?"

I turned my head toward where he was pointing and stated, "That's cool. They've got all the church member's names on the wall."

When he looked at me, I could see that he was serious as a heart attack, "No! Those are people who didn't tithe last week."

I was in disbelief. "For real?"

"Yes. This is a segregated church. Let's get out of here."

I kind of chuckled when he said that and quipped, "A segregated church in Mexico? They're all Mexicans here, why would they be segregated? There's no white folks here, no black folks here. They're all Mexicans."

He was almost frantic at this point, "No! Look inside. The women go on one side and the men have to sit on the other side and they can't talk to each other while they're in church. This is one of those old, old-time, stuck-in-the-way-back-yonder churches, and we do not want to put our kids in here. Now get in that van!"

David couldn't get out of there fast enough, because he realized he was in a church that was trapped in a mindset of religious thinking. It was a church that thought the way to get into heaven was by being more religious and having more rules and more regulations. The MV of religious thinking suffocates people by heaping upon them rules, regulations, and constraints that the Lord never intended them to bear. You don't have to pay money or be locked into man made rules to be a Christian. Your Christianity is by God's grace; your salvation is a gift.

GOD MAKES ALL THINGS NEW

If you have ever spent any time in the heart of Mexico, you are more than likely to run into the Lady of Guadalupe and the celebrations on Our Lady of Guadalupe Day. Tens of thousands of people converge on a shrine in Mexico where people try to pay for their sins by self-inflicted pain. It is a tragic thing to watch. I've watched and cried. I've watched them get on their hands and knees—crawl, crawl, and crawl—hoping to get to church so that they can have their sins absolved. They have cut and bruised their knees and hands on the way. These people believe that punishing their body appeases their god.

That's not what is in the Bible; that's not the Jesus I serve. You don't have to pay for your sins—your sins have already been paid for by Jesus Christ. That was what Jesus was trying to tell the Pharisees, "Guys, you're making up a bunch of rules and regulations and this has nothing to do with a relationship." You see, God is all about relationship! He wants to have a relationship with you. Yet, we think it's not possible, because our mind is infected with the MV of religious thinking.

Jesus was telling the Pharisees, "You cannot put all these rules and regulations on these people. It will not work." And it would not work today. You can't come to church and have an old mindset. You can't come to Visalia First (the church I pastor) and say, "Well, this church is going to be like my last church..." because you would be very surprised! We believe that the Lord's mercies are new every morning! The Bible says in Lamentations 3:22-23, "Because of the Lord's great love we are not consumed, for His compassions never fail. They are new every morning; great is Your faithfulness." If we get stuck in the old methods and ways of the past, we're going to miss what God is doing today.

> **YOU DON'T HAVE TO PAY FOR YOUR SINS. THEY HAVE BEEN PAID FOR BY JESUS ALREADY.**

One thing I want you to realize is this: If you can restore your mind toward what is good, God can bestow His blessing on you. You know the devil fights for your mind. Some of you think the Devil has you physically tied up, but it's your mind that he loves to get all tied up. He starts putting thoughts in your head like *What are people thinking about me?* When thoughts like this come, he is starting to tie up your mind.

Let me ask you something. What does it matter what people think about you? Are you going to let what people might or might not be saying about you keep you from enjoying life to the fullest? The reason you have low self-esteem is because it's in your mind. If you want to lose weight, it's in your mind. If you want to be a happy person, it's in your mind. Happiness is a choice! You've got to get your mind fixed.

FIX YOUR MIND

How do you fix your mind and get rid of the mind virus of religious thinking? Well, you've got to get your head out! You know when a baby is born, the baby comes out head first—if you can get your head out, everything else will follow. If you can get your head out, the rest of your life will line up. You've got to get your thinking straightened out. Here are seven words that will change your life: "As one thinks, so shall they be" (Proverbs 23:7, *paraphrase*).

If you think you're going to be successful, you're going to be successful. If you think you're going to be a failure, you're going to be a failure. If you think you're going to be something, you're going to be something! You can think your way into a better future! Isn't that good news?

Life is a series of births. Consider when a child is in its mother's womb. As the child gets ready to be born into this world things become increasingly uncomfortable for the mom—the birth pangs are more frequent and intense. The mom says, "Get that baby out of me." But the baby is just having a good time hanging out there in the womb. There is free air-conditioning, free food piped in, and no bright lights messing up the sleep. That baby is fine for a while. But then what happens? After a time, that baby has outgrown its present space.

> **IF YOU THINK YOU'RE GOING TO BE SUCCESSFUL, YOU'RE GOING TO BE SUCCESSFUL.**

In the same fashion, some of you have outgrown your present space and you're starting to feel very uncomfortable in this life. You're starting to curse the darkness and groan. You think, "God, why am I going through all this pain?" God simply explains, "I'm preparing you to go to another dimension my child. You have outgrown your present dimension. I'm taking you somewhere and I'm getting you ready."

We know this is true, but we still cry out, "Okay, Lord, but it hurts!"

We have to keep in perspective that what we're going through now is taking us to the place God wants us to be. The process is like when we were physically born. When we're being born into this world our head and shoulders squish up. It hurts to leave the womb and come out into the bigger world. Like a midwife, God pulls us out of the place we presently reside. While we're trying to stay settled in and comfortable, God is pulling, pushing, stretching us to come out and to live in the light. He has us moving in to a brand new dimension, developing a new way of thinking that is less religious and more relational. The old religious thinking will diminish while the new truths Jesus gives will increase.

In order to get ready for new truths, we sometimes have to let go of the old truths that have fulfilled their purpose for the season of life we were in. Think back when you started school as a child. You learned some things in the first grade; then, you learned different things in the second grade. Each year we were in school we learned something new. Year after year, we layered truth upon truth. However, in order to get to the place where God is taking you, you will need to know and be prepared to lay aside elementary truths for deeper, more challenging truths that transform you into His servant.

WHAT WE'RE GOING THROUGH NOW IS TAKING US TO THE PLACE GOD WANTS US TO BE.

Take for example how the law of gravity works. We all feel and recognize the power of gravity. If I step off a cliff, I'm going to fall down into a deep ravine. If I throw a rock up in the air, it is going to fall back down to the ground. I live under the effect of the law of gravity, but did you know that there is a law that overrides the law of gravity? It's called the law of aerodynamics.

On December 17, 1903, Orville and Wilbur Wright made their first sustained, controlled flight in a powered aircraft after many failed attempts. Since that time, vast improvements were made to aircrafts. Now you can fly 30,000 feet above the ground and defy the law of gravity for hours. The law of gravity has to give way to the law of aerodynamics. That's the way it works.

Some things you learned when you were young have to go when you become an adult. Even though some of childhood things are good, they give way to better things as we mature. Everything has its season. Now you are in a different season. God is teaching you different things. If you have an old mindset, you're not going to be able to go where God is taking you.

The week that Jesus was going to be crucified, He told His disciples to get everything ready for the Passover. Everybody knew what that festival meant. They had been celebrating the Passover for hundreds and hundreds of years. They were going to get the wine that represented the blood, they were going to get some bitter herbs that represented the bitter experience coming up out of Egypt—they were going to get everything Moses told them to get when they did the Passover. Each of the disciples could tell you the meaning of the elements in the Passover meal, but Jesus was about to add an entirely deeper meaning to those elements.

Jesus called all the disciples together and He grabbed the cup and handed it to one of them and said, "Boys, take and drink this. This is the blood of My new covenant."

With a look of shock and disbelief, one of them may have wanted to speak up and say, "Whoa, whoa, whoa, that's not what Moses told us. Moses said to put the blood on the doorpost which meant the death angel had to pass over."

But Jesus explained, "I am bringing you a new covenant. You have to get rid of the old truths in order to be able to live in the new truths. My blood is going to cover you from death." He then took the bread, broke it and said, "Take, eat. This is My body which is going to be broken for the remission of your sin."

> **IF YOU HAVE AN OLD MINDSET, YOU'RE NOT GOING TO BE ABLE TO GO WHERE GOD IS TAKING YOU.**

Again, the disciples cried out "Whoa, whoa, whoa, Jesus. That's never been in our theology before. Because when we broke bread back in Moses' covenant, the bitter herb was representing getting out of Egypt. No, Jesus, you're changing things."

Jesus explained again, "If you don't get rid of the old truths, you're not going to be able to go with the new thing that I'm doing. I am freeing you from a deeper bondage, the bondage of sin and destruction." He was telling them, "You cannot pour new wine into an old wineskin. You've got to get ready for some new truths by getting rid of the mind virus of religious thinking." If you're not ready for it, you'll miss what God is doing in your life.

Some of you have a new life on the inside of you, but you've got the old life on the outside of you. Have you ever seen a real smart woman with a really outdated hairdo? Sort of freaks you out a bit, doesn't it? If she's really smart, why is she wearing a 1970s hairdo? Some things are like that. You can be new on the inside, but old on the outside; or you could be new on the outside, but old on the inside. Jesus says, "Get ready for the new thing I will do in you. Get rid of your MV of religious thinking, then you'll be ready for what I want to do in your life."

Old truths have to give way to new truths in order to maximize the moments of your life. Then you can be ready for the new thing that God is doing.

TEENAGE RELIGIOUS THINKING

I was a typical 19-year-old boy. Do any of you know what a typical 19-year-old boy is thinking about? Is it getting an education? Is it wondering how to be successful? No. The one thing a 19-year-old boy thinks about is simply—girls! When I was a teenager and before I was saved, I remember a day that changed my life. It was a day where I was first and foremost thinking about girls.

I woke up that morning and smoked a joint. Then, I went to work and did my job. A lady walked in. I was still about half high from smoking weed. She walked up to me and said, "You want to come to church?"

I let my eyes kind of glance up and down at her and said, "You have any ladies at this church?"

She looked at me with a sweet smile and said, "Oh yeah, a lot of ladies."

I thought for a minute and then said, "Good looking ladies?"

"Lot of good looking ladies." She smiled ever so sweetly. "Plenty."

"For real?"

She replied, "For real."

Being half high from the joint, I never protested or questioned it. I believed the lady.

After I got off work, I went to church with her and to my extreme disappointment there were only two or three ladies there. "She lied" I thought, but I stayed through the service anyway. When the worship service was almost over a skinny preacher looked at me and said, "Hey boy, you look like you need some prayer."

"Yeah?"

He told the others, "Let's pray for him. You ready?"

"Yeah, I guess so." I then made the sign of the cross, patted my chest, kissed my fingers and gave him a peace sign. I had seen someone do that on TV one time and didn't know what it meant.

I said aloud, "Okay. Now I'm ready."

Let me tell you, those folks prayed for me and they were hooked up to some kind of power I had never seen before. I had been to church, but the church I had attended didn't pray like that. By the time they got done praying for me, I was born again. I was filled with the Holy Spirit. I got on the phone and called my momma. I said, "Momma, I got the Holy Ghost" (We only had the *King James Version* of the Bible and not the *New International Version* yet, so we referred to the Holy Spirit as the Holy Ghost in those days).

She said, "You got what?"

I told her again, "I'm born again, Momma, and I got the Holy Ghost!"

She said, "Okay, boy."

After that night, I started living right. I stopped drinking and getting high. My mom started telling her friends about how I had changed. One day, she told the Sunday School Superintendent in the other church and said, "My boy got the Holy Ghost."

"What?"

She stated again, "He got saved and filled with the Holy Ghost."

The Superintendent asked, "What church is he going to?"

"He's going to that Assembly of God church over there."

He looked at my mom and told her very sternly, "Tell him not to do that, because the Holy Ghost was only here to start the church in the early days. It's gone now. We don't need to be filled with the Holy Ghost anymore."

Momma called me up and said, "Hey boy. Superintendent says that was already gone and you don't need the Holy Ghost."

I couldn't contain myself, "Momma, it's all over me. I've been high on other things, but I've never been high like this before. I'm high as a kite. It won't leave! I've got the Holy Ghost."

The things I had learned earlier in life—my religious thinking mind virus—suddenly was replaced by the new things God wanted me to learn.

You know, the Wright Brothers did more than help defy the laws of gravity when they soared above the ground. They also changed the way in which we see our world. Back then, people traveled across the land in every direction—the world was two dimensional. You crossed lines that separated one town from another town. But with the coming of airplanes and human flight, you could see the world from high above and the boundaries below disappeared. People who had flown in a plane gained a new perspective, but it was always hard for them to explain the wonder of flight to people who had never flown.

I often say that a person with an experience will never be at the mercy of a person with an education. People who had never flown could never dismiss the joy the Wright brothers experienced by being up in the sky in an airplane. The Wright boys knew flight was possible. They knew that it was an amazing way to travel because they had experienced it firsthand. In the same way, you cannot tell me that God does not heal people today—I have experienced it. You cannot tell me there isn't any Holy Ghost (Holy Spirit)—because He is real, and His filling did not pass away—I have experienced it.

When you are working a garden or field you always clear away old debris, pull weeds, and turn over the soil. That daily labor is needed for good seed to take root, plants to grow strong, and for the crop to reach harvest. Well then, consider religious thinking as a mind virus of decaying thoughts, weeds and hard soil that chokes spiritual growth. It can rob you of a rich harvest of peace, love and righteousness. Be prepared to learn from God, and to allow His new, deeper, richer truths to take hold in your mind.

BE PREPARED TO LEARN FROM GOD AND ALLOW HIS TRUTHS TO TAKE HOLD IN YOUR MIND.

If I had to write up a spiritual coroner's report on what kills growth and maturity in the Lord, then I'd say the number one mind virus is religious thinking. I've seen it wreck churches, ministries, neighbors, friends and family. It builds fences in the mind where Christ would offer an open range of creativity and grace; it keeps people on the ground of mediocrity when God wants them to fly boldly and in power. Religious thinking is a particular strain of mind virus that has roots in MV families that we are about to explore—fear, pride and despair. It is by no means the only strain. What is afflicting you? Let's find out; let's address the infection before it kills your mind. Time and choices are precious.

FURTHER DIAGNOSIS

1. Be a spiritual coroner for a moment: What mind virus do you think is hurting most people today? Religious thinking? Financial Stress? Medical Worry? What?

2. How would you distinguish between the religious thinking MV versus a godly thought defending righteous behavior?

3. Can you recall an incident where you have had to let go of an elementary truth to understand God in a deeper way?

4. Is there someone in the Bible that you relate to who was plagued by a religious thinking MV?

5. What do you believe is the first step in letting go of a religious-thinking mind virus?

FILLING YOUR PRESCRIPTION

1. Today, there are a lot of mind viruses going around; there are plenty of _____ _____ people loaded with venomous poison.

2. The most destructive mind viruses today is _____ thinking.

3. The MV of religious thinking _____ people by heaping upon them rules, regulations and contraints that the Lord never intended them to bear.

4. If we get _____ in the old methods and ways of the past, we're going to miss what God is doing today.

5. If you can get your _____ out, everything else will follow.

6. Here are seven words that will change your life: "_____ _____ _____ _____ _____ _____ _____."

7. If you think you're going to be _____, you're going to be successful. If you think you're going to be a _____, you're going to be a failure.

8. In order to get ready for new truths, we sometimes have to let go of the old truths that have fulfilled their purpose for the _____ of life we were in.

9. Old truths have to give way to new truths in order to _____ the moments of your life.

10. Consider religious thinking as a mind virus of _____ thoughts, weeds and hard soil that choke spiritual growth.

CHAPTER 4
THE FEAR VIRUS

"Never let fear determine who you are. Never let where you came from determine where you are going." — Constantine 'Cus' D'Amato, American Boxing Manager, 1908-1985

EVERYBODY HAS A NICKNAME...and even those pesky biological bugs do. The best known virus by name is the flu or what the medical folks call Influenza. It's a virus that has an incredible capacity to quickly spread from one person to the next, and the capacity to mutate into different varieties from year to year. When you think of viruses you are usually thinking about the flu. At one time or another people contract the flu. It's the kind of virus that nations take seriously. That is why they set up medical centers to research and distribute vaccines to protect their citizens. Every year the Centers for Disease Control and Prevention (CDC) headquartered in Georgia coordinate the distribution of new vaccines to immunize millions of Americans from the nasty, sneezy, wheezy, flu bug.

Having served as a pastor in many different communities and in visiting ministries worldwide, I've noticed a few thought-corrosive MV families. These are negative, destructive and crippling thoughts that share similar family traits, but carry a distinctive strain of attack in hurting you. One family of MVs that spreads like wildfire and easy to spot is rooted in fear. This kind of MV has various strains in the form of anxiety, fretting, nervousness, and cowardliness. It is seen in anxiety

> ## ONE FAMILY OF MVS THAT SPREAD LIKE WILDFIRE ... IS ROOTED IN FEAR.

over finances, fretting over the loss of relationship, nervousness when called to lead, and cowardliness to do what is right in the face of intense peer pressure. It's an MV inhibitor—it inhibits you from growing in God's grace and having peace in any circumstance. Fear deeply paralyzes, quickly spreads, and often changes into new strains. It is a family of MVs that inhibit the spirit of a person to achieve, listen, and adapt. We've all been beat up by those haunting, nagging, irritating MV voices from the family of fear? Does the sound of the internal voices listed below sound familiar to you?

- *If she knows what I did in my past, she will reject me.*
- *He's going to yell at me for speaking the truth.*
- *How am I going to make rent this month?*
- *How am I going to pay for this medical bill?*
- *They're going to hate my creation.*
- *In the end, am I going to be alone?*

The religious thinking MV epidemic is partially associated with fear. The fear of doing worship in a different way, the fear of praying aloud (or quietly), and the fear of sharing Christ in a public venue are examples of how fear takes different forms.

KEEP YOUR EYE ON THE BREAKER

Ever see someone throw the breaker at the Rockefeller Center or for the National Christmas Tree Lighting? It's an amazing site to see something like a major building or tree sparkle in a shower of light! It's beautiful, it's a lot of power, and it costs a lot of money to run that power into the light bulbs.

When I was a child, it was a scary thing to throw a breaker with that much electricity. As I grew older, it became easier to throw the breaker. I knew it wasn't going to hurt me. I knew that in order to obtain desired results, I had to throw the breaker and then keep an eye on how long the electricity was running. If my dad came home and discovered that no one was watching how long the breaker had been left on, we ran the risk of losing a lot of revenue.

MY MIND CAN BE LIKE A BREAKER BOX FOR MY LIFE.

My father had a lot of freezers and cooling units that ate up electricity. I learned an important lesson here: My mind can be like a breaker box for my life. What I decide to "thrown on" or "throw off" has a cost associated to it. One of the most costly of all MV groups is the family of fear. If I leave a current of fear running through my mind long enough, it will drain the energy out of my imagination, drive and organization. It's the kind of mind virus that leaves one with a bill of regret that has to be paid down the road. In contrast, a wise decision generates revenues of blessing.

Here is another truth about throwing the breaker switch in our thought life: Each of us controls the direction of our destiny by the thoughts we cultivate into attitudes and actions. When you walk into a dark room the first thing you usually do is find the light switch and turn it on. Doing this keeps you from stumbling around in the dark, which keeps you from seriously injuring yourself. In a similar way, our mind can be overcome with darkness and in those moments we need to find the light switch in our

> ## EACH OF US CONTROLS THE DIRECTION OF OUR DESTINY BY THE THOUGHTS WE CULTIVATE INTO ATTITUDES AND ACTIONS.

brain. Left unattended in the darkness, our MVs cause us to stub our toes and stumble on to the cold floor—it ruins our attitude and cripples our walk to do what's right.

Lisette Norman (commonly known as "Peace Pilgrim") walked more than 25,000 miles in the U.S. to promote peace and the value of thinking positively about the future. She once said, "If you realized how powerful your thoughts are you would never think a negative thought."[8] Her simple, profound message has inspired people all over the world. It's a good lesson for us—thinking positively illuminates our mind to see God's blessings and to believe in His promises.

FEAR OVERRUNS THE MIND

Have you ever been around someone with a bad attitude? Everything that comes out of their mouth is doom, despair and agony—you often want to yell at them and say, "Enough! Isn't there anything good going on in your life? Why can't you be thankful? Why can't you see the good that comes from the pain and sorrow?" Your attitude depends on what you choose to

---

8. Peace Pilgrim, *Peace Pilgrim: Her Life and Work in Her Own Words,* (Ocean Tree Books, 1992)

allow yourself to think about and act upon.

When our anxiety is uncontrolled we begin to imagine many different scenarios that are played out in the theater of our mind. You can't sleep. You can only watch the plays you've created through your whacked-out, run-away fear. One week it's the play *What If They Blame Me?* The next week it's *How Will I Survive* followed by a special night of fright: *Will I Ever Find A Mate?* You get the point. All the worry consuming your brain cells is fueled about possible outcomes from real and imaginary things that have happened or will happen. When that fear runs wild it smothers and blankets everything—you can't and don't want to push yourself anymore, take a risk or explore the horizon.

Have you ever heard of the ivy plant called *Kudzu*? It's a plant that loves to overrun everything in the forest. It was introduced into the United States from Japan during the 1800's. During that time, the U.S. government paid farmers to plant Kudzu because it was a fast growing ground cover. What they didn't realize was that when left to itself, the ground-cover vine would grow at the rate of one foot each day. It would coil, climb and cover anything in its path—trees, abandoned cars and even houses. The Kudzu of fear is just as prolific in filling your mind.

BEING BOLD

The chief quality of fear is it keeps you small (remember, it inhibits you from being bold, courageous, creative and happy). When we embrace internal messages of fear, we deny ourselves blessings that are directly in front of us. We become so immobilized by worry that we miss the opportunity to lead, serve, bless and be blessed. In comparison, if we challenge our external pressures with courage, we unleash hope and faith.

THINKING ON WHAT IS POSITIVE SHAPES WHAT WE PLAN AND HOW WE ACT.

In the past, the American writer Norman Vincent Peale was highly criticized for his power of positive thinking ideas. Yet, as it turns out, he was right on the money. Today science is catching up with what the Bible has been teaching for years. One passage reads, "For God has not given us a spirit of fear, but of power and of love and of a *sound mind*" (2 Timothy 1:7, *NKJV*). Thinking on what is positive and praiseworthy shapes what we plan and how we act.

When the Church was in its infancy and just taking root in Jerusalem 2,000 years ago, there was a very bold man named Stephen. This guy was sold out in following Jesus. He was out in the open, bold, making the Pharisees of his day nervous because of his testimony for Jesus. These religious bigwigs were very upset with Stephen. They eventually stoned him to death (Stephen was the first martyr for Christ recorded in history). They did not realize that Stephen's courage to boldly proclaim Jesus regardless of the cost had already left an impression on the people in Jerusalem. The Church grew rapidly after his death.

RISK IN FAITH

When I was growing up, I sensed in myself an ability to think outside of a problem. My dad passed away when I was seventeen and I had to grow up quick. The six months that followed his death were the worst in my life, but in the midst of it all I discovered some latent abilities about myself. One quality within me was a natural capacity to be a risk-taker. Even as I witnessed many of my contemporaries being hijacked by their emotions and problems, I found that I had courage to go beyond the safe zone. I could lay aside my problems and push myself to explore new frontiers. Over the years my boldness to take risks has been magnified by my faith. Today, I believe anything is possible with God. When Christ is the focus of your heart and you have a direction in life you enter a world of adventure.

People often wonder how and why they cannot take a risk. It's a mind virus that is standing in the way. We wrestle with our thoughts: *What will people think of me? What if I fail? Why should I ruin my comfortable life?* Whatever the excuse, I think the best antidote against these MVs is simply to take the risk. Are your nervous? Try talking to God about it. Are you feeling afraid? Remember His promises in the Bible. Are you unsure of direction? Seek out God's counsel in Scripture and through wise counselors. Whatever you need to do, get out there and do it! It's worth the risk.

My wife Karen and I once made one of the most life-changing decisions we had ever faced. We decided we would move from California to Texas and start new careers. Easy—right? Hardly, we were in our 40s and that's a season of age where you generally want to stay put—be in a place where everyone knows you. She struggled with it a bit more than I did. Finally my good friend, Danny Robinson said: "If you make a mistake you can use your faith to get out of it." Wow! Isn't that a freeing concept? If you can believe that faith gets you in then believe it gets you out, too…

because the faith is built upon a spiritual Rock—God Himself. Take this truth to heart and you can rid yourself of riskless living.

There's a great quote that I enjoy from the 20th Century American writer and essayist Logan Pearsall Smith. He wrote: "What is more mortifying than to feel that you have missed the plum for want of courage to shake the tree." You can miss the opportunity and adventure if you don't take the risk to shake the tree for the fruit that is obviously there. Ask yourself: *Why are you hesitant to pursue something new? Why do you feel what you are seeking won't happen or won't work? What is stopping you from acting in faith? What does the Bible say about faith for believing in good results when the circumstances seem overwhelming or too hard to handle?*

BORDER PATROL OF THE MIND

The best defense against paralyzing fear is simply to patrol your mind on a regular basis. For fifteen years, Karen and I lived near San Diego, California. During that time, we helped a lot of missionaries across the border in Mexico. My friends and I have gone across the busiest border crossing on the planet hundreds of times. However, I still feel nervous each time I make the trip. I often contemplate, *What if they won't let me back in? What if I get stuck in a Tijuana jail? How will Karen get me out?*

Fears, being some of the most common mind viruses, have an incredible way of consuming our thoughts. When I let my mind dwell on the "what ifs" of crossing the border, there was no end to the worries. My fearful thoughts were limitless! At the bottom of all those disturbing thoughts was a single fact: When I crossed the border, I was at the mercy of one person—the Border Patrol Agent. That scary person had the authority to prevent me from returning to the United States, my home and my family. Obviously, I certainly don't see these guards as the enemy. I know how important the Border Patrol agency is for the nation's security. It is established to filter out people trying to illegally enter the United States. If the border is unguarded, the U.S. is unprotected and vulnerable to the drugs and violence that plague some parts of Mexico and Central America.

FEARS HAVE AN INCREDIBLE WAY OF CONSUMING OUR THOUGHTS.

The Border Patrol is a metaphor for agents who protect our minds. An unguarded mind is vulnerable. Fear MVs take advantage of vulnerability with great speed and impact. These viruses tunnel their way into our thoughts and are smuggled in through the guise of being practical concerns. We have to be on guard all the time that practical thinking does not degenerate into panic thinking. If fear penetrates your mind on a certain project, in a relationship, while you are under pressure or even feeling lonely...it will replicate into hundreds of bad scenarios. Fear plunges our common sense into the pit of cynicism; it converts our imagination into a factory of anxieties, and, it shackles our faith.

THERE ARE ONLY TWO TYPES OF PEOPLE IN OUR LIVES: THOSE WHO MAKE DEPOSITS AND THOSE WHO MAKE WITHDRAWALS.

There are only two kinds of people in our lives: those who make deposits, and those who make withdrawals. We have to choose whom we allow in our lives. I've placed a few people as Border Patrol agents at the door of my mind and imagination. I've surrounded myself with people who are smart, wise, perceptive, and mature. They are the sounding board for my ideas and a hedge of protection for my fears. I talk to them about virtually everything I plan to do. When I get an idea or read about a strategy I think will work, I run it by them. Those agents of God's wisdom and grace help me recognize thoughts that may be alien or dangerous. I can appreciate the patrol agents in my life...they're defending the borders of my mind and life.

These people are worth more than gold to me, but the best Border Patrol agent in my life is the Word of God. It's the source of truth and the best filter of everything that passes through my mind. The Bible says, "Finally, brothers and sisters, whatever is true, whatever is noble, whatever is right, whatever is pure, whatever is lovely, whatever is admirable—if anything is excellent or praiseworthy—think about such things" (Philippians 4:8).

This is the Paul's P-4-8 Standard (a phrase coined by Rev. Kevin Gerald when referring to this passage). It is important to evaluate our thinking: Is it "right?" In other words, does it agree with God's truth in His Word? Is it "pure," "lovely" and "admirable?" As we've seen, truth should always be coupled with kindness. Jesus came "full of grace and truth." That's how we should relate to people, too. Finally, everything we think, say and do should bring praise, glory and honor to God. Solomon agreed with Paul. He gave us this advice: "Be careful what you think, because your thoughts run your life" (Proverbs 4:23, *NCV*). Truly, the Word of God is our mind's best Border Patrol. Read it. Memorize it. Believe it.

I've found the Word of God and wise counsel to be a powerful combination to keep MVs from running wild...especially ones born out of our fears. In Jesus' most famous message, the Sermon on the Mount, He began six points in His message like this: "You have heard it said, but I say to you...." He doesn't want anyone to miss His emphasis on what will follow because Jesus was reminding His listeners of things that they'd heard for years. Now He was giving them a radically different way to think about life. If I paraphrase chapter 5 of Matthew, the introduction to all six of these life-changing truths, it would sound like this: "I want you to replace the thinking you previously acquired with a higher, better way of thinking." All of us—young and old—have acquired our share of *stinking thinking*. Jesus invites us to rip these thoughts out of our minds and replace them with new and better ones. When it comes to dealing with our fears, the Lord helps us to become overcomers—people of courage and boldness.

If you spend time with people who are higher thinkers (people who are wise, discerning, and creative), you can begin to retrain your mind. Centuries ago, King Solomon recognized the positive and negative influences of relationships. He wrote, "He who walks with wise men will be wise, but the companion of fools will suffer harm" (Proverbs 13:20, *NASB*). Now you might ask, "Where can I find wise people?" Good question. We need to look hard to find people who have internalized the grace and truth of the Scriptures and live by the power of the Spirit. Regrettably most of the people I know are lower thinkers (foolish, stubborn and unimaginative)." Higher thinkers are rare. When we can't speak with them face-to-face, we can at least read books and articles they've written. There is simply no excuse for not growing in God's wisdom. Your responsibility is to find sources of wisdom and soak your brain in them! Only then will

YOUR RESPONSIBILITY IS TO FIND SOURCES OF WISDOM AND SOAK YOUR BRAIN IN THEM.

the mind viruses be exposed; only then will you identify the good and right thoughts to replace them.

FAITH DRIVES BOLDNESS

The heroes of the Bible were average, everyday people. Many of them faced mind virus fears that we experience today. The power of those worries (both imagined and real) always leads to some kind of paralysis, petrification or neutralization—right into the arms of the god of "playing it safe at all costs." God doesn't want us to play it safe, He wants us to risk. I am not talking about being reckless (remember, it's good to get wise advice and good counsel from the Word of God), but I'm talking about the risk that comes from faith in the One who is calling you to action.

If we let our fears govern our lives we become hiders, howlers and hoarders—we run away from our bullies, we howl about how bad things are, and we hoard things because we're afraid we will be without resources on a rainy day. My friend Will is a communications professional. He once shared a painful story about how his father suffered from Obsessive Compulsive Disorder (OCD). It is a condition where the mind gets warped over a particular passion that often appears at the outset as something good and healthy. It may be a passion for plants, cats, dogs, birds, cars, bikes, shoes, boxes, dresses, dolls, toys, or sports memorabilia. When fear is mixed with passion, the person with the hobby begins to lose perspective in what they are doing or collecting. Will recounts:

I never expected my father George would be afflicted with OCD. After my mother died in '88, my father began to reconnect with childhood passions—one passion involved his love for pigeons. At first the hobby was a positive thing because it gave him purpose and joy. Sounds good—right? Well, when I moved back home to be close to my dad in his old age you can imagine my surprise when I saw close up (after being away for many years) the condition of his home: the broken walls, the lack of running water in the kitchen, one bathroom without a functioning toilet, and enormous clutter in the home—everything showed a profound neglect. I thought, *What happened?* Then I saw multiple pigeon lofts in the backyard with hundreds of little eyes looking back—I was stunned. The harmless little hobby that started with a handful of birds had multiplied into hundreds of birds with some being housed in the garage. It was like living in a suburban bird estuary—the retirement village for pigeons! In later conversations (that quickly turned into arguments), I found my dad mentally entrenched and emotionally bonded to acquiring more birds and protecting the ones he had, even at the expense of his home, finances, health and walk with God. *The pigeons had become the reason for living.* He was always afraid someone on his street would eventually complain and that the city would try to take his birds away—an event that in his mind would mark the end of his life. Fear twisted his priorities.

George's story is not uncommon from a spiritual point of view. When fear is in the driver's seat you end up taking some awful side roads to your destinations in life. How many of us have fears that come from thinking we can't live without something (e.g., pet animals, jewelry, shoes, money, homes, cars, sports, food, art, traveling, etc.) or that we can't live without someone (e.g., boyfriend, girlfriend, husband, wife, child—you name it). The MV fear of loss leaves a terrible scar on people.

REMEMBER GIDEON

In the book of Judges there is the story of Gideon. He was an average Israelite who did an extraordinary thing—he freed his people from the tyranny of the Midianites. The Midianites and their allies had an army so vast that the Israelites could not even count them. The Israelites cried out to God for help, and God decided to use Gideon. When the Angel of the Lord appeared before Gideon, he greeted the surprised Israelite by saying, "The LORD is with you, mighty warrior" (Judges 6:12). Was Gideon that brave? Well, the angel thought so; God thought so.

THE MV FEAR OF LOSS LEAVES A TERRIBLE SCAR ON PEOPLE.

Gideon was threshing wheat at the time when the angel appeared, but it was not on a threshing hill (a place where you'd throw the wheat into the air to separate it from the chaff). He was threshing wheat in the winepress at the bottom of the hill in an enclosed room. Why? Well, maybe Gideon was being practical by hiding his harvest, and maybe he was afraid. He had good reason: the Midianite boys never left the Israelites anything. Times were tough.

Gideon was still unsure he was hearing from the Lord so he asked God for three proofs—miracles—and the Lord did not disappoint. Once Gideon was sure it was the Lord calling him to service, Gideon acted on his faith. He took the risk of putting his life on the line by choosing to fight against the Midianites. His first objective was to rally and recruit his neighbors to fight. After some success in getting recruits, God suddenly informs Gideon (I'm paraphrasing), "You have too many guys for Me to deliver you from the Midianites. You need to take a smaller force and trust Me to take care of the rest." Gideon did as God asked and the count of his final army was 300 men versus the Midianite army—an army so big that it could not be counted. In the end, Gideon's tiny army defeated the Midianites even though the odds seemed against the Israelites. It's amazing that Gideon's MV of fear didn't get the best of him. Can you imagine if Gideon had listened to those negative voices? *Hey Gideon, God did not speak to you. Hey Gideon buddy, do you really think you stand a chance beating these guys? Hey Gideon, if you're so brave why are you threshing wheat in a winepress?* Can you imagine if Gideon's troops had listened to their destructive voices? *Hey, this guy Gideon is taking you to your death. Do you really expect to win with 300 guys?* But Gideon and his men overcame the fears. Gideon listened to God's nudge and message, and took the risk to win a great victory for the Israelites.

The fear MVs can be beaten with wise counsel, God's Word, and the courage to step out and take a risk (trust). One of the best encouragements on this wisdom came from David himself. Here is what he wrote: "Do not fret because of those who are evil or be envious of those who do wrong..." and later adds "Refrain from anger and turn from wrath; do not fret—it leads only to evil" (Psalm 37:1, 8). Great advice for how to live each day.

FURTHER DIAGNOSIS

1. Recall the times you were anxious or worried and describe whether it helped or hurt you.

2. What is the difference between legitimate concern for another person versus fretting over their welfare and health?

3. What's your greatest fear? Why?

4. What do you think is the most debilitating effect from being anxious or worried?

5. What did Jesus say about worry?

6. What is the most memorable verse in the Bible addressing your fears and worries?

FILLING YOUR PRESCRIPTION

1. My mind can be like a _____ _____ for my life. What I decide to "throw on" or "throw off" has a cost associated to it.

2. Lisette Norman, "If you realize how _____ your thoughts are you would never think a negative thought."

3. People often wonder how and why they cannot take a _____. It's a mind virus that is standing in the way.

4. Danny Robinson said: "If you make a mistake you can use your _____ to get out of it."

5. You can miss the opportunity and adventure if you don't take the risk to _____ _____ _____ for the fruit that is obviously there.

6. We have to be on guard all the time that _____ thinking does not degenerate into panic thinking.

7. There are only two kinds of people in our lives: those who make _____, and those who make _____.

8. I've placed a few people as Border Patrol agents _____ _____ _____ of my mind and imagination.

9. The best Border Patrol agent in my life is the _____ _____ _____.

10. If you spend time with people who are _____ _____ (people who are wise, discerning, and creative), you can begin to _____ your mind.

CHAPTER 5

THE PRIDE VIRUS

"Nothing can stop the man with the right mental attitude from achieving their goal; nothing on earth can help the person with the wrong mental attitude." —*Thomas Jefferson, Former U.S. President, 1743-1826*

MIND VIRUSES, AS WE'VE SEEN, are basement voices. MVs are negative intruders into our thoughts and attitudes. They poison our motives and harm our relationships with the people we love. Mind viruses that often prove difficult to uproot and replace are ones hardened by pride—the attitude of self-sufficiency and entitlement—that blinds a person. Pride weakens humility, a quality God esteems which helps us view the world in a sober way. Our spiritual immune system operates out of a humble mindset, because that virtue sees the material and spiritual worlds in a sober light before God.

We know that physical addictions rewire the brain (substances like alcohol, cocaine, and methamphetamines). These drugs, through continued use, form new neural pathways, making the effects of these substances seem completely normal. The person who attempts to stop their own addiction will feel sick and abnormal. Addictive behaviors involving food, sex, gambling, and shopping have the same effect on the brain. Over time, what began as a single bad choice, leads to a terrible physical and emotional bondage.

Mind viruses, like addictions, are learned behaviors. Keep in mind. That a single negative thought does not immediately destroy a person's life. Yet, given enough time, that one corrupt thought replicates into many destructive thoughts, then actions, then habits and finally a lifestyle. Pride is often the catalyst that prompts us into an addiction. Among the MV families, it is especially difficult to extract because a proud attitude blinds one from taking action to fix the dysfunction.

I remember the first time my sister and I tried smoking. I was eight years old; my sister Novelice was seven. We thought we were so grown up and cool in trying to smoke. We were proud. We took a couple of *Swisher Sweets* cigars to our clubhouse with some other boys. I liked the name of those cigars, and the name perfectly described the smell…sweet. I couldn't wait to light up. I took a few puffs and I gagged! My friends had the same reaction. Suddenly, we looked at each other with this question running through our minds: *Why do grown-ups enjoy this so much?* A couple of my friends got sick. Yet, our pride did not let us reject the practice. We still saw smoking as the cool thing to do. We only needed more practice.

By the time I was fifteen, I was regularly smoking cigarettes. I enjoyed it and used it to relieve stress. Do you see the transition? Smoking began as a horrible experience, but *I learned to enjoy it. Something that was sickening to use eventually became normal for me.* It was the same with drinking beer. I vividly remember the first beer I ever drank—it was awful! I made one of those bitter-beer faces. I hated the taste. My pride kept telling me that cool people drank beer, so I kept drinking it. I convinced myself that I could handle it and enjoy it. Over time, I learned to savor it. Smoking and drinking became integral parts of my life. I couldn't

SOMETHING THAT WAS SICKENING EVENTUALLY BECAME NORMAL FOR ME.

imagine life without them! It took something dramatic and wonderful to push those things out of my life and replace them with something far better. I met Jesus and experienced the wonderful grace of God! When I met Christ at the age of nineteen, He miraculously replaced both of those learned behaviors with new delights and desires.

Smoking or drinking are some of the most obvious vices that point to mind viruses controlling our behavior, but they're not the most dangerous. The most dangerous ones are those that invade and infest our lives without our knowledge. Smoking and excessive drinking are so easy to spot––they have a very clear pathology. You can't miss them. Yet, how do you identify a mind virus that is subtly sabotaging relationships, destroying happiness, and opening the doorways of the mind to bitterness and despair?

Pride distorts thinking in subtle ways. Pride says you are entitled to be rude toward others (because you're being honest); entitled to blame others (because you're getting justice); and, entitled to resist admonishment (because you are being true to yourself). Do you see how pride and humility are opposing forces? Humility says it is wise to be gentle toward others (because Christ's love is seen); it is wise to be forgive our neighbor (because God forgave us first); and, it is wise to listen to correction (because we grow in obedience to Him).

CATCHING A BOASTFUL, STIFF-NECKED ATTITUDE

Let me remind you that a mind virus is usually something you caught from somebody else. Just as we catch a viral infection from another person, we get our stinking thinking from others as well. People have debated for years whether the evils of the world are from "nature or nurture." I think it's a powerful combination of both. The Bible tells us that the natural human heart is self-absorbed and against God—in a nutshell, that's pride. Coupled with this problem is the fact that we live in a fallen world with other fallen people. We're sponges soaking in our environment—and some of us have lived in very toxic environments!

Like people with a weakened immune system, we have a predisposition to catch mind viruses. When our pride takes hold it makes us susceptible to a terrible range of thoughts. We catch

A MIND VIRUS IS USUALLY SOMETHING YOU CAUGHT FROM SOMEONE ELSE.

specific MVs from social interaction. We feel hurt by someone we trusted. If our hurt is not addressed, then our pride creeps in and morphs into self-pity, an entrenched fear, or a hardened resentment.

Contracting a MV of pride can even occur by simply watching people interact with each other through TV, on radio, and face to face. One of my favorite pastimes is watching people. We all like to do it. The people in Hollywood figured this out decades ago and have made billions by creating the aura of celebrity knowing that everyday people want or imagine having the same degree of beauty, freedom, money and power at their fingertips. We have so many reality shows today, because the TV network executives know we love watching other people react to awkward situations and difficult people. These shows offer a perverse comfort (even an attitude of superiority). We see dysfunctional behavior acted out on TV and we begin to think that such behavior is normal—we begin to open ourselves to these destructive MVs. If a destructive MV is already rooted in our mind, we discover that watching such a TV program is strangely comforting. Our twisted thoughts begin to rationalize the verbal abuse and vicious physical assaults: *I am not the only one ripping into my spouse. Look at those people—they're worse. I never try to hit the one I love. I just tell it like it is, I cuss up a storm, point my finger, and make them miserable for challenging me.*

You don't need a television, however, to watch others interact. Just look around you when you're at the mall or a sporting event. Notice how people relate to their friends, family members, and strangers. Most of us are shrewd observers of human nature. We can identify particular patterns of behavior and categorize people with our mental filing systems. We're especially attuned to watch those closest to us. If you stay around them for a lengthy period of time, you'll pick up their mannerisms. This is called borrowed thinking. It's not who we really are and the perceptions didn't originate with us, but we have borrowed the trait from someone else.

MUCH OF THE THINKING WE'VE PICKED UP THROUGH THE YEARS IS A BORROWED PACK OF NONSENSE.

Let me make a statement that may offend some people: Much of the thinking we've picked up through the years is a borrowed pack of nonsense which makes us miserable. I believe this is absolutely true for some (if not most) people on the planet. For example: Have you ever caught yourself acting like someone negative only to solemnly promise you'd never act like that again? That's the effect of a mind virus. You didn't want to catch the MV, but spending time with that person infected your mind and heart, and it showed up in your actions. It is easy to gravitate to and imitate a boastful attitude because the MV encourages boisterous, loud, controlling and manipulative actions. A prideful person may even appear successful from a worldly viewpoint. They may have money, power, religious thinking superiority, and charisma, but they lack what God esteems—humility.

INHERITED MVS AND SELF PERCEPTION

All MVs feed off our broken and unfulfilled expectations. Men and women entering into marriage often carry presumptions regarding how the other one should act in a relationship. The new groom's parent's behaviors and values may be miles apart from the bride's. For instance, her father may have pitched in to do cooking and cleaning, so she expects her beloved new husband to delight in washing dishes. But his dad never saw the inside of the kitchen, except to raid the refrigerator late at night. After the honeymoon, they get to their apartment, and she is mystified that he doesn't even offer to help her cook dinner. And after they eat, he wanders off to the den, leaving her with all the dirty dishes. She feels unloved, and her accusations make him feel terribly disrespected. Both of them have a mind virus where pride sets up expectations and demands that produce actions and verbal exchanges that are destructive and demeaning to the other. Their blended MV mutation will poison their marriage from the beginning!

We are shaped in childhood by what we observe in our parents. If your parents had an unhealthy relationship, you almost certainly have deeply entrenched fears and defenses that can sabotage relationships. You may grow up thinking your perceptions and actions are completely "normal" toward your spouse when in reality it is distorted and destructive. You may have excused your attitude and actions by saying, "That's just the way I am. Take it or leave it." That excuse is about the dumbest mind virus on the list! You're saying that you value your comfort zone and walls of self-protection more than you love the other person. In actuality, you're lazy and your callous attitude will drive your loved ones away.

Our self-perception is formed in relationships. As children, we absorb messages from our parents and family members, and internalize these messages to determine if we are loved, competent, creative and successful. If warmth, optimism and wisdom saturate our development in childhood then our self-image becomes strong and resilient in adulthood. The opposite is also true. If negativity, negligence, and abandonment barrage our development in childhood then our self-image becomes weak and unstable in adulthood. Our self-perception is like a building we have created to house our personality. If our building is dilapidated and weak, we always wonder when the walls are going to come crashing down on us. We live in fear, anger, and self-protection. We manipulate people instead of loving them simply because we don't know what love looks like in relationships. We live our entire lives in a shaky building, and we can't envision any other way to think, feel and act. We don't believe we're special in any way, and we don't have any real hope for a glorious future. We're afraid to dream because we're sure we don't deserve anything good to happen to us. We try to dominate people in a display of raw power to feel significant. Living this way feels completely good and right because our minds tell us this is the only game in town. It's not.

> ### WE'RE AFRAID TO DREAM BEECAUSE WE'RE SURE WE DON'T DESERVE ANYTHING GOOD TO HAPPEN TO US.

Life can be different. You can carve out a new identity, hope, and future. To make this radical change, you have to look beyond your five senses. If you don't like where you are in life, change your thinking today to ensure a better tomorrow. We don't have to face the challenge of change alone. The message of the Bible is that God loves us so much that He paid the ultimate price to demonstrate His love and claim us as His own. If you're a believer, you're a perfect candidate for change. The Spirit of God lives in you. The Creator of the universe is speaking to your spirit and invites you to co-create with Him. If we change the way we think, we can change the way we live. It's time to silence those basement voices in your life.

OBSERVE AND LEARN

Wisdom comes from many different sources. There is wisdom in listening to wise counselors, and in absorbing good teaching from the Bible. There is also wisdom in being a good student of observation—studying the failures and success in the lives of other people. Sadly, we often fail to learn valuable lessons from the easiest method of all: simple observation. Rather, we take the hard route—we personally make life-altering mistakes. Our observations then come from our own failures and successes.

Of course, we naturally take on the attitudes and perceptions of the people we hang out with on a daily or weekly basis. For this reason, I encourage people to make sure they spend plenty of time with people who are wiser, smarter and nobler. One day, when I was seventeen, I was getting high. I was on Blueberry Hill (yes, that was the actual name of it, just like the 1950s version of the Fats Domino song) with four of my dope-smoking friends. This was in my "BC" (Before Christ) days. Our conversations revolved around the familiar topic that we expounded on numerous times: "Why are all the pretty girls so stupid for not going out with cool guys like us?"

As I sat there holding a joint in my hand and taking a drag, I had one of those "Ah ha!" moments. It was a revelation! As I looked around at my friends, I realized that I was the smartest one in the circle. I was hanging out with people who were dumber than me! Though I hadn't come up with the term yet, I suddenly realized the source from where all the mind viruses were coming. I finally realized how MVs were making me intellectually, socially, and spiritually sick. The company you keep can be a breeding ground for MVs or a hatchery for good thoughts.

After that day, I began to look for people who were smarter than me. I found that the wisdom they offered was like having a roadmap—life could be navigated in a better way with wisdom. I also discovered that having wise people in my life kept me accountable to walk humbly before the Lord. That combination of wisdom and humility began to shape my ability to prioritize values in the light of God's Kingdom. I was learning to make distinctions between what was truly important over what might appear urgent.

The deciding moment to change my company of friends and pursue better things happened decades ago, but it's still one of the best choices I ever made. It led to other great decisions because I was determined to avoid settling for a mediocre life. If I kept hanging with the same friends and smoking dope, I was headed for something far less than what God wanted for me. I decided to push for more, reach higher, and take some risks. Since then, I've put myself in situations that stretch me. Setting high goals and going for them has called out the best in me. It has forced me to seek the advice of very gifted people. I've learned tons from them.

THE RIGID RELIGIOUS THINKING MV

When I became a Christian and started following Jesus, I didn't immediately find wise people in the Church. The people I came across were very religious. I was impressed with how much Scripture they knew and how many rules they could recite. They had all the right words down and knew about all the places where they wouldn't go. But there was another trait I noticed—one that I assumed was good, right and normal for devoted Christians: *a critical spirit*. These people could find fault with an ice cream sundae! Many people today would laugh at the rigid rules and strict conformity taught by some churches in the past, but it wasn't funny at the time. It was spiritually deadly.

Obviously, some religious thinking MVs can be traced to fear, but there's a variety of religious thinking that is spawned from pride. We know that mind viruses are more often caught than taught, and that can be true for a follower of Christ. You may be hanging out with people who are poisoning your mind. I did that for years. I hung out with small-minded church people who felt it was their job to force people to fit into their mold. We were like the Pharisees who constantly harassed Jesus. We were a miserable bunch of people. We demanded that people jump through our hoops and fit into our mold. We were miserable and we made others miserable.

I'm very thankful God brought some people into my life to challenge my religious rigidity and judgmental spirit. I'm equally glad the modern Church has relaxed a bit and is spending more time teaching people about a relationship with Jesus instead of demanding compliance with religious rules. In the wrong hands, the truth of the Gospel can be twisted and the message co-opted into a harsh, condemning moralism. Grace, then, is lost and evil reigns. If you have a religious mind virus being fueled pride, get some help. Find people who genuinely love Jesus, obey Him, and have hearts filled with gratitude. Get into a Bible-believing, Spirit-filled church where your heart feels at home. Don't stay around dead, empty, poisonous religion. If you stay, you'll pay a price and your family may pay an even greater price.

PRIDE TAKES US AWAY FROM THE TRUE CORE OF OUR FAMILY.

Whereas MVs rooted in fear paralyze, MVs rooted in pride petrify. *Pride renders the heart stone dead, turns the mind to lead, and strangles the soul from being fed.* The Bible is clear: "He has shown you, O man, what is good; and what does the LORD require of you but to act justly, to love mercy, and to walk humbly with your God (Micah 6:8, *NKJV*). Pride takes us away from the true core of our faith. It creates fights over petty issues and blinds us to what is truly important.

I recently asked Pastor Rose, an older minister, to compare Christianity today to what it was like in the 1940s and 1950s. He was around when churches had great healing crusades and big tent revivals. Thousands upon thousands of people were divinely healed. These events were birthed in the Holiness Movement. These people had great hearts. They wanted to get as close to God as they could and as far away as possible from the world.

I asked Pastor Rose if he ever longed to go back to those days when truth and morality were more sharply defined by Christians. He was a wise man. He smiled and said, "I prefer living in today's culture."

I asked him to explain further.

He replied, "In those days, we spent a lot of time getting people in great shape for heaven. We wanted them to look like they belonged in heaven. Today, the emphasis has shifted. The Church today is focused on getting more people into heaven rather than getting people in great shape for heaven. Simply put, years ago we got less people into heaven in better shape, but today they are getting more people into heaven. I've lived through both periods of time, and I prefer the latter."

My first days as a follower of Christ were spent with people who tried their best to get me into great (at times even expecting perfect) spiritual and moral shape. I think people meant well, but they took things to the extreme. I was talking to a friend, one time, who told me about being raised in a strict Pentecostal church and home. Each day she had to repent of her wicked ways. Otherwise, should she die in her sleep at night, she was bound to go straight for Hell. Now let me ask you: How much wickedness is there in a 6-year-old little girl? At that age, all she knew were rules: no going to movies; no bowling; no make-up; no dresses above the knee; and, definitely, no dancing! No, No, No! Basically, if something was fun, it would send you to eternal damnation. Heaven was created for God and His children, but the slightest disobedience against God's laws, as explained by this church's teaching, would mean *you* were making a decision to spend eternity in Hell. Going to Hell was an ever-present threat. There was a lot of fear and manipulation taught in the church she attended. Years later, when she disagreed over what was being taught by the pastor and other adults, she would get a very stern "Thus says the Lord" preceding a rebuke or admonishment. It was a tactic to make their declarations and will seem to be divinely inspired, and therefore to be obeyed without question. All this manipulation was heaped on a person so they could try to be more holy and more worth living as a child of God.

As I grew in my faith, I stumbled upon a passage of Scripture that set me free from trying to get all of the outward stuff right. Moved by the Spirit, the Apostle Paul wrote,

See to it that no one takes you captive through hollow and deceptive philosophy, which depends on human tradition and the elemental spiritual forces of this world rather than on Christ. Such regulations indeed have an appearance of wisdom, with their self-imposed worship, their false humility and their harsh treatment of the body, but they lack any value in restraining sensual indulgence (Colossians 2:8, 23).

The truth of this passage hit me––I'm never going to be holy enough to merit God's approval with my own performance. The Gospel is full of grace for those who realize they can't measure up. The rules and regulations have value to demonstrate the holiness of God, to show us how short we fall, and how much we need God's grace. And after we trust in Him as our Savior, the rules give us guidelines to show us how to live in glad obedience. But following the rules aren't—and never were meant to be—leverage to twist God's arm so He'll accept us. That's a complete distortion of the Gospel of grace!

I WILL NEVER BE HOLY ENOUGH, BUT I CAN GET HUNGRY ENOUGH.

Today, I often combat prideful religious thinking with this statement: "I will never be holy enough, but I can get hungry enough." Grace produces a hunger to know, love and follow Jesus. God doesn't look at our outward appearances. He's looking at our hearts. He's thrilled when He finds someone who has a heart to love and serve Him. Once I understood the importance of having a hungry heart for more of the things of God, I entered a whole new realm of love, joy and freedom.

I also realized some things aren't worth our time and energy. We need to focus our attention to loving Jesus, and be cautious of focusing our attention to our worries and the petty games people play. For instance, I remember a lady who had a daughter with numerous body piercings. The mother wanted me to talk to her daughter about these piercings. I thought, *Why should I care if she pierces her body? She can pierce her body until she looks like a walking hardware store, and I wouldn't tell her she was a sinner for doing that! God loves her. That's what she needs to hear from me.* Recognizing how to invest the time and resources God gives each of us (the important) from the irrelevant or petty (the urgent) helps us from falling into some mind virus traps or contracting a bad MV from someone loaded down with toxic thoughts.

NON-NEGOTIABLES, NEGOTIABLES AND PREFERENCES

As a leader of a mega-church, people often want me to take sides in their disputes. I've realized I need to be careful where I step. There are religious-thinking landmines—emotional explosives—set to go off inside people who are nurturing petty resentments and proud arguments in opposition to God's mercy and grace. I have learned that I may have an opinion about a subject, but if the issue isn't crucial then my little ol' opinion may stir up more trouble than I can resolve. It is important that we all learn how to determine what's non-negotiable (a core belief and reality that defines our faith), what's negotiable (an issue where Christians can disagree how something is delivered, appears or is applied), and a preference (personal styles). Let me illustrate:

Preferences	Negotiables	Non-Negotiables
• What we wear	• Rapture	• Christ
• Tattoos	• End times	• Holy Spirit baptism
• Body piercings	• Speaking in tongues	• Bible as the Word of God

I'll die over the non-negotiables of our faith. You can never talk me out of the crucifixion and resurrection of Jesus Christ. The resurrection of Christ sets Christianity apart from all other world religions and philosophies. Christianity is the only one that can claim its founder rose from the grave. It is a proven historical fact: our entire faith is built upon Jesus defeating death and rising from the grave.

Another non-negotiable is the presence and power of the Holy Spirit which saved my life. In my youth there was a time I was headed down the wrong road. A group of people prayed for me and I was filled with the Holy Spirit. Many people have different opinions about the role of the Spirit today, but I'll die defending the truth of His life-changing power. God's Spirit knows the deepest parts of our inner being and works to transform us to be more Christ-like in our actions and thoughts.

The last non-negotiable for me is in divine healing. I've seen it so many times. There is unmistakable and irrefutable evidence of God's power to restore, reverse and renew. At one point, I was sick and prepared to leave the ministry. God came down into an apartment building and divinely healed me. You'll never be able to tell me divine healing "doesn't happen today" or "it's all in your head." It happened to me. I experienced it first-hand. A person with an experience is never at the mercy of a person with an abstract theory.

There are some things that are non-negotiable, but many more things that are negotiable. I may try to persuade people to my point of view, but I won't die to defend my opinions. For instance, some people say you can't smoke or drink and go to heaven. I don't smoke any longer, but smoking is not going to send you to hell. (It may make you smell like you've already been there, but it won't keep you out of heaven).

Another negotiable is speaking in tongues. Some say it is old-fashioned and not relevant for today. Based on I Corinthians 14, I respectfully disagree. I enjoy my prayer language each day, but I also accept Christians who may not practice tongues in their daily life.

Some of the strongest convictions usually occur over discussions about the "end times" of the Church. People wonder what the Rapture, the Second Coming, the Beast, and the Antichrist are all about. Some believe that Christ could return today and rapture us into the clouds with Him and then The Great Tribulation would begin. Other Christians have a mid-tribulation or post-tribulation viewpoint. I have my preference, but frankly, I don't care what you believe about the Rapture. I'll arm-wrestle you over my understanding of Scripture, but I'm not going to die for a seven-year theory of the tribulation.

It's amazing that people get so worked up—angry, demanding, and defensive—over things that just don't matter. But that is pride for you, a boastful heart makes it tough to listen, serve and love. Many preferences are driven by a person's culture, age, and ethnic background because preferences are styles and the forms we choose to wear, use or apply. Personally, I don't care what kind of clothes you wear. I tend to like funky clothes, but many religious people don't like my selections. It's not worth getting in a snit over someone's wardrobe choices. There are much bigger issues in life.

I don't have any tattoos or piercings, but if you do, it doesn't bother me. Many people think body art is a wonderful form of self-expression. That's cool. I'm not going to lose any sleep over it. But I caution people to be careful and think before they get them. Some employers won't hire someone with tats or studs, so the choices you make today may have an impact on your career choices.

Food choices are preferences over which many people hold widely differing views. Some people don't eat any meat; others only eat organic fruits and vegetables. The point here isn't to find reasons to condemn and alienate. The problem arises when we make our personal preferences non-negotiable demands. That mindset creates divisions and explosive verbal exchanges! That's not the kind of relationship Jesus extended toward people who were different in appearance and culture. He didn't make a big deal of preferences. He looked beyond the superficial and valued the heart of the individual.

When our pride makes a mountain out of molehill, we may find people who agree with us, but we also offend and push way some people Jesus wants us to love. In your own heart, try to know what is non-negotiable, negotiable or simply a preference when worshiping and fellowship with other people. Don't let a mind virus generated from personal pride obscure the bigger picture of loving your neighbor in the name of the Lord.

FURTHER DIAGNOSIS

1. How do mind viruses operate in a similar way to substance abuse behaviors?

2. Have you ever caught a bad mind virus from someone? Explain.

3. How can you identify the toxic, prideful thoughts that are so deeply entrenched in your perceptions and habits?

4. When you have suffered from a religious mind virus, was it related more to fear or pride?

5. When it comes to your faith, what is non-negotiable, negotiable or a preference?

FILLING YOUR PRESCRIPTION

1. Mind viruses, like addictions, are _____ behaviors.

2. A single negative thought does not immediately _____ a person's life. Yet given enough time, that one corrupt thought replicates into many destructive thoughts, then actions then habits and finally a _____.

3. The most dangerous ones are those that _____ and _____ our lives without our knowledge.

4. Much of the thinking we've picked up through the years is a _____ pack of nonsense, which makes us miserable.

5. If you don't like where you are in life, change your thinking _____ to ensure a better tomorrow.

6. The company you keep can be a breeding ground for MVs or a _____ for good thoughts.

7. Where MVs rooted in fear _____, MVs rooted in pride, _____.

8. I'm never going to be holy enough to merit God's approval on my own _____.

9. "I may never be holy enough, but I can get _____ enough."

10. It's important that we all learn how to determine what's _____ - _____, what's negotiable, and a_____.

CHAPTER 6

THE DESPAIR VIRUS

"Despair is a narcotic. It lulls the mind into indifference."
— *Charlie Chaplin, British Actor, 1889-1977*

I OFTEN ASK PEOPLE, "Why is it that some people flourish, but others don't?" It seems some people have a touch that turns everything into gold, and other have a touch that turns everything into ashes. It's all in the way we think: *As you think, so shall you be!* You can set the stage for your failure and success by what you plant and nourish in your mind.

People who flourish are people who think flourishing thoughts. People who don't flourish have negative and destructive thoughts. If I were to ask you, "Do you want a terminal case of cancer?" You would look at me in horror and scream. Of course you wouldn't want that sickness. No one in his right mind would want that to happen. People, however, quickly jump to terrible conclusions when they experience any pain or discomfort. They assume the worst. Fear clouds their perceptions. Their hope vanishes like mist on a warm, sunny day.

When fears mix with failed expectations it often results in depression. For many people that depression can be severe enough to imprison their dreams. It hurts so much inside that they can't muster the strength to go outside. They feel alone, unloved and unwanted. Despair may take root in the loss of a loved one, in a damaged relationship, a shattered career or in the loss of financial security. Like the deadly *Ebola* virus in the physical world, despair is a MV that is incredibly lethal to the soul. In its worst stages, despair will raise an accusatory finger against anyone and lay blame on others for the setbacks or failures suffered in life. Unlike the MV of pride that aggressively accuses others in moments of failure, the nature of despair is that it retreats, implodes, sulks and seethes bitterness toward those who are perceived as causing the hurt. Pride tends to be explosive and eager to take revenge; despair tends to be listless and hungry to escape reality. Pride shows disdain of others with a similar weakness or failure, but despair finds a twisted comfort in others sinking in the same mire. If you want to see a zombie of the mind then find one who is consumed by deep despair—that person is barely alive.

REJECTING THE "DIE"-AGNOSIS

A number of years ago, during a routine examination, a doctor informed me he was fairly certain I had cancer. He was one of the most respected doctors in Dallas, Texas. I looked him straight in the eyes and replied, "That's impossible."

He showed me the report of the blood work and repeated, "You need to come back for more tests, because I think you have cancer."

I didn't take my eyes off him. I asked, "Doc, do you have anyone in this building who can give me a massage? You're stressing me out, and I need someone to work the kinks out of my shoulders."

He looked at me like I was an idiot and remarked, "You don't get it, do you? I just told you that you probably have cancer, and you want me to refer you to a physical therapist!"

I simply refused to believe him. He put me through six months of evaluations. One day while the nurse was preparing to do another blood test on me, the doctor rushed into the room. He stopped the nurse from prepping me. He told her, "There's no need to do the procedure. He doesn't have cancer."

I probably should have felt relieved, but I was actually upset. The doctor told me to get dressed, and that he would meet me in one of his examining rooms. After a few minutes, he came in and sat down. Before he could say anything, I barked, "Doc, you've got to quit doing this to people! You told me six months ago that I had cancer. I'm a man of faith. I take news like that to God, and He always works it out for me. But what happens to a person who has no faith? What if you tell them they have cancer, and they can't handle that kind of news? What keeps them from running up all their credit card bills and living the high life because you told them they were going to die? Or worse, they may sink into despair and commit suicide."

Despair is lethal. It can block out the truth of God's infinite love and power, because the person can't see beyond their own personal pain.

Through the voice of a highly skilled physician giving me his assessment of my body's health, he passed along a virus of doubt that tried to infect my mind. However, I refused to let it. I hung on tightly to the wonderful truth that in Christ all things are possible and God healed me (see Mark 10:27; Philippians 4:13).

Author, speaker and life coach Tim Storey used an inspiring illustration years ago about the power of our faith to drive away doubt and despair. One of the ways to get a thousand channels on your television is to have a huge satellite dish installed outside your home. Installation, though, is tricky. If you don't get the dish positioned exactly right, you get fuzzy reception. If you want a particular station, you can point the dish in a certain direction. If you hit it just right, you get a clear signal. That's a metaphor of spiritual reception. I need to position my personal faith to the *All Things Are Possible Network*. When I hear bad news, I send it through the filter of God love, His power, and His Word.

> OUR THOUGHTS DETERMINE OUR FEELINGS, PERCEPTIONS AND OUR CHOICES.

A WOMAN OVERCOMING DESPAIR

Our thoughts determine our feelings, perceptions, and choices. The messages we confirm in our hearts shape everything about us. Even when the external circumstances are negative, we still have a choice to have our internal messages filled with hope, courage, and faith or with sorrow and despair. Matthew describes Jesus' encounter with a woman who had been sick for years. Her faith overcame the despair of her situation.

Just then a woman who had been subject to bleeding for twelve years came up behind him and touched the edge of his cloak. She said to herself, "If I only touch his cloak, I will be healed."

"Jesus turned and saw her. "Take heart, daughter," he said, "your faith has healed you." And the woman was healed from that moment (Matthew 9:20-22).

For more than a decade, this woman had spent all her time and money in her attempt to get well. Can you imagine a life-threatening disease for that long? She had plenty of reasons to be discouraged or be filled with despair. She spent all of her money on doctors, but the only thing she received from them was more hopeless information.

Fortunately, her internal dialogue was positive. Her hope and faith fought against the difficulties of her situation. She told herself, "If I only touch His cloak, I will be healed." A lot of people were touching Jesus that day. Everyone around Jesus had a different agenda with different needs and wants. Yet, this woman was determined to reach Jesus. She had faith that if anyone could heal her condition, it was Jesus of Nazareth. Her internal dialogue wasn't concerned about power and prestige. She refused to allow a mind virus of doubt, discouragement and despair to hijack her life. Her focus was on Christ, on the Nazarene of hope, healing, grace and power. Through the crowd, she reached out to Jesus, touched the edge of his cloak, and years of suffering ended instantly.

FOCUSING ON THE GOOD

Let me share a story about the power of focusing our mind on the positive. Ladies, let us say you are sitting in an expensive hair salon in Beverly Hills, California. You've chosen this salon because it's where many celebrities get their signature styles. It's world-renowned and has a reputation for impeccable service. As you look around the room at all the people enjoying the attention, you notice your stylist coming toward you with a pair of shears in his hand. You've never met him before. He has an emotionless expression in his eyes. There is a half-smile on his face. His attitude and demeanor is impossible to read. Suddenly, panic grabs your heart. *Is this guy going to style my hair or butcher it?* For a moment, you wonder whether you can change your mind about this appointment. Making a mad dash to the door seems appealing! Yet you stay. Why? Because your focus is *built on the expectation* that no matter how the stylist appears that he will remain a professional, uphold the good brand of the salon, and perform wonders on your hair and appearance.

Now let's say that you can see all the events of your stylist's life prior to his arrival at the salon. Honestly, his day couldn't have gotten much worse. He was barraged by unexpected hassles, pains, and bad news. In the morning, his wife told him that she didn't love him and wants a divorce. When he got in his car to leave for work, the battery was dead. Later, the bank called to inform him that several checks had bounced, and the penalties were exorbitant. On the way to work, he was involved in an auto accident and it was his fault.

Knowing how his morning unfolded, let's go back to him standing behind you holding a pair of sharp scissors. He's ready to take your hair in his hands. Let me ask you a question: Do you want him to take out his frustrations on your hair? No, of course not. Do you expect him to greet you with a smile and act like he's happy? Do you expect him to do his best to make you look great? Sure you do because you are paying him to be professional. That's your focus and expectations. He is there as a stylist. He is there to do his job.

Now, what might the stylist be thinking after working through a difficult morning of setbacks? Your stylist has a simple (if not difficult) task. He knows he is there to serve you and the clients. His focus is on making you look fantastic. He knows he has to refrain from his self-talk about being the angry victim. He must come across as a gracious, skilled, and personable stylist (his boss expects that too). He must choose to style your hair with a good attitude. He must provide you with great service and an outstanding new look for your hair; he must make you and his employer happy. The excellent care he offers (regardless of the turmoil in his personal life) is connected to gaining a hefty gratuity, praise from you and the boss, and maintaining his credibility as a world-class hair stylist. He earns his reward by focusing on his craft.

Changing focus is something you and I do (or need to do) many times each day. It is something we expect others to do, too. It may be hard, but it's necessary. There are no excuses. God has given us the power and wisdom to choose our attitudes. We should never doubt our ability to switch focus. Learning to choose your focus produces tremendous rewards in your life. Each day you can choose to focus on things that bring discouragement or those that produce peace. Adjusting your focus when faced with discouraging news is a first line of defense against the MV of despair overrunning your mind. Having a thankful attitude focused on the good and praiseworthy offsets the power of a mind virus.

GOOD THOUGHTS AND GOOD SPEECH

Jesus' famous story of The Prodigal Son says that the younger brother wasted his life living on the wild side, but then "he came to his senses." At that point, he began to see and think very differently. He mentally bought a ticket to a new destination. He said to himself, "I will get up out of this wretched place and go back to my father's house." He could have simply stayed in the pig pen and wallowed in the mud of depression and sorrow. Some people get comfortable with that mud, but they aren't pigs, they are people created in His image. The Prodigal Son changed his focus. He had to leave the mud. He began to apply the P-4-8 Standard. Let's look at this great passage again and consider one additional verse:

Finally, brothers, whatever is true, whatever is noble, whatever is right, whatever is pure, whatever is lovely, whatever is admirable, if anything is excellent or praiseworthy, think on such things. Whatever you have learned or received or heard from me, or seen in me—put it into practice. And the God of peace will be with you (Philippians 4:8-9).

This passage provides a measuring stick to evaluate our thoughts. Are our thoughts poisonous mind viruses or do they reflect the love, forgiveness, wonder and purposes of Christ? Paul goes on to use his personal life as an example of refocusing on what is good. At one time he had zealously persecuted Christians (even was witness to Stephen's killing). Yet, through God's Spirit and Word, Paul was transformed daily into a man committed to sharing the love of Christ with others. His thoughts, words and habits changed.

A heavenly mindset to what is right and good comes through in our speech (words are an extension of our thoughts). The P-4-8 Standard acts as a filter between your mind and your mouth—you begin to choose clear words that exhort, inspire and counsel. In our culture today, it seems there are very few filters in communication. People will say anything they want to say to anyone at any time without tempering such expressions with wisdom and love. Our unbridled tongues degrade society and destroy relationships by using words that tear down, wound and punish. Ironically, some people view a harsh tongue as being an honest one, which is not always true. Besides, truth goes farther and renews the inner parts of a woman or a man when the one speaks with wisdom and love.

Even in radio, TV, cable and the Internet it seems that angry people get the attention and ratings. People seem to delight in name-calling, accusation and rage. Everyone who listens and watches becomes infected with this anger, and it can produce frustration, discouragement and despair. Oh, some of what these on-air commentators say may be right, but the way they say it is a long way from the model of Jesus. It is true that the Lord corrected people from time to time, but always out of love. Eventually, He died for those who hated and opposed His message of life and hope. Integrate the P-4-8 Standard in your daily living and remember Paul's example in verse nine. Refocus on God. His goodness will transform your speech to strangers, neighbors and family.

UNDERSTANDING ABUNDANCE

Today, there are many people with financial mind viruses and distortions over how to create and understand the nature of wealth. It is amazing how many people fall into a quick and deep despair when their finances go awry. Now you may be a person who never had much money. Most people on the planet can say "Amen" to that. It's not uncommon when you don't have much money to blame your financial woes on your parents, your education, your spouse, your kids, your previous employer, the world financial crisis or bad luck. We can always find someone to blame! However, if you carefully analyze what's holding you back, you may discover that money trouble has followed you throughout your life, no matter what your environment has been. You may be reinforcing your misguided beliefs while talking with others by complaining, "I can't ever get ahead. Something is always against me."

Do you realize God is a God of abundance? If you come from a poor background, it may be harder for you to believe it, but it's true. God is the Creator of the universe and the ultimate giver. Everything we have and everything we are comes from Him. He isn't stingy. He delights in blessing His children. Moses reminded the people of Israel, "But remember the LORD your God, for it is He who gives you the ability to produce wealth, and so confirms His covenant, which He swore to your ancestors, as it is today" (Deuteronomy 8:18).

I used to think abundance was available only for a lucky few. At some point, though, I realized it's part of the overflow of God's love and available to everyone. Abundance is yours for the asking. But we need to be very careful. In our culture, greed is a destructive epidemic and can easily degenerate into depression when our schemes do not materialize our way. Many people

> **ABUNDANCE IS YOURS FOR THE ASKING, BUT WE NEED TO BE VERY CAREFUL.**

feel entitled to riches, pleasure, comfort and lavish possessions. We get into debt over our heads because we refuse to say no to whatever we crave. We need to ask ourselves a very important question: *"What's our greatest treasure?"* If power, prestige, pleasure and possessions consume our thoughts (delight us when we have them and discourage us when we don't) then it's a sure sign these things have taken God's rightful place in the center of our lives.

Too many for too long have focused on money and material things as trophies. There's more to life than accumulating goods, having power over people, or seeking fame. I have found Jesus to be far more valuable than all of that! If we want to find real meaning and love, we have to identify and ruthlessly kill the mind virus of greed and entitlement which, when left unchecked, can easily morph into despair when the money runs out and toys are gone.

To be detached from the lure of money, shift your focus to Jesus and the life-fulfilling values in Him. Power and prestige also must take a backseat to loving the Lord. If you find your purpose in living for Christ on this planet, plenty of money, authority and acclaim will arrive without you being consumed by it. Detachment is the awareness that you are not defined by your bank account, people's opinions, or the latest gadget. We're meant for more, much more, and Christ helps us to see that true potential.

Ask yourself a piercing question, "Has money, power, comfort, and success brought me the satisfaction I believed it would?" If you feel like you must have these things to be happy, then you're too attached to them. Greed isn't limited to a particular economic class. Poor people can be consumed with the desire for *some*, and rich people long for *more*.

If we stop and pay attention, we may realize God has already poured out His riches of abundance on us. Psychotherapist and author Dr. Wayne Dyer tells this excellent story about two fish in the ocean to illustrate how important it is to perceive how wealthy we are already in Christ.

"Excuse me," said one ocean fish to another, "you're older and more experience than I, and will probably be able to help me. Tell me: where can I find this thing they call the ocean? I've been searching for it everywhere to no avail."

"The ocean," said the older fish, "is what you are swimming in right now."

"Oh, this? But this is only water. What I'm searching for is the ocean," said the young fish, feeling quite disappointed.[9]

---

9. Wayne Dyer. *You'll See It When You Believe It.* (New York: Morrow Paperbacks, 2001). p. 158.

You and I have been immersed in God's vast ocean of blessing and abundance. You don't have to keep trying to find it—you're there! Take a moment to read the Book of Ephesians and you'll see how blessed you are in God. Truly letting this reality sink into your heart can give you a thankful heart in all situations and a natural resistance to despair.

TRUST THE WORD OVER EMOTIONS

Despair and discouragement are combated with a daily renewing of our focus, drawing on good thoughts and wise company, and listening to what the Word says. It is keeping our eyes on true wealth—our relationship with Jesus. God can heal us and help us rise up out of anything that brings us despair. When we affirm the truth and power of God to heal, amazing things can happen. As I've read the Bible and seen God in action in people's lives, I'm convinced He wants to work in powerful ways—to comfort the afflicted and show His awesome glory!

The problem, of course, is that our minds and emotions often scream that the Bible isn't true and God doesn't really care about us. At those times, we have a choice: to depend on our perceptions and feelings or to trust in God's revealed Word. We have to believe, live and walk beyond our five senses.

Our senses can throw us off God's path. My friend, Floyd Westbrook, offered this illustration when he was speaking in 2012 at a Bible Breakfast in Visalia, California:

> One of two things is controlling your life: your will or your feelings. Both are always present, but only one can be in control. It is like a locomotive. In front of the train, the engine is pulling cargo to the desired destination. At the end of the train (at least in the old days) is a caboose. The caboose doesn't have the power to pull anything, and it doesn't carry any of the load. It's there for the man in the back who watches out for the end of the train. For many people, their emotions are the engine, and their will is stuck in the caboose. They careen from one dramatic or depressing feeling to another. It shouldn't be this way. Our will should be the driving force in our lives—no matter what our feelings may be. Paul wrote to Timothy, "For God did not give us a spirit of timidity, but a spirit of power, of love and of self-discipline" (2 Timothy 1:7). When we live according to our will instead of our emotions, we have a spirit of power, love, and self-discipline. That's the way God designed us to live, grow, and thrive.

Anytime we allow our feelings to lead our lives, we're headed for an unfulfilled and disastrous life.

If we live solely by our emotions, our will becomes weak. However, if we live by our will, we are fully aware of every feeling. But those feelings won't dominate us. Many people (including Christians) live under a dark cloud of painful emotions: sorrow, dread, resentment, and hopelessness. There's nothing wrong with any emotion. They are God-given indicators to show what's in our hearts. The solution to these feelings, isn't to become numb and passive but to ask, "What's going on in my soul? What in my heart needs attention?"

Asking these questions is an act of a sensible will over turbulent emotions. We then make choices—sometimes hard and courageous choices—to live by God's truth. We trust in His love and cling to His promise for our futures. Gratitude is a choice we can make every moment of every day. We may not feel thankful, but if we choose to give thanks and focus on God's goodness and greatness, our feelings (our caboose) will eventually follow the engine of our will.

OUR SIXTH SENSE

Feelings aren't an enemy. They can serve very good purposes. If you're in daily conversations with God, your spirit is awakened to the God of the universe. Your spirit can connect to your sixth sense—your spiritual sensitivity. We sometimes think of heaven, the angels, and the supernatural world as "somewhere way out there," but that's not the case. The spiritual world is another dimension all around us right now. It's not distant, and it's not unapproachable. The "cloud of witnesses" cheering us on are as close as each breath we take. And God is always watching over us. He's not checking out some other galaxy. He's as intimate and interested as a mother with her child.

As our relationship with God grows closer, we are more in touch with His mind and heart. We pick up on His cues more readily. Spiritual perception isn't just for monks or super-saints. This experience is for every beloved child of God. Soon, we learn to recognize the voice of God like we recognize a dear friend's voice. A part of us comes alive. Our "spiritual knower" is certain, beyond a shadow of a doubt, about the things that are of God. Gradually, these convictions grow, and they become the firm foundation of our spiritual lives. We are more confident in God and His purposes. Even when we experience difficulties and delays, our certainty isn't shaken. Paul described this kind of rock-solid confidence: "For I am convinced that neither death nor life, neither angels nor demons, neither the present nor the future, nor any powers, neither height nor depth, nor anything else in all creation, will be able to separate us from the love of God that is in Christ Jesus our Lord" (Romans 8:38-39).

Despair and depression often arise when we have forgotten or have never seen our true identity and purpose in God. Our hope in God is rooted in knowing how deeply He loves each of us in spite of our failures. We are His children with a great role to play in life and eternity. If you know these truths, you become highly resistant to negative circumstances and feelings. When your eyes are on the "Pioneer and Perfecter" of your faith—Jesus Christ—you can weather any storm.

When the medieval writer Dante wrote the *Inferno*, he described hell as a place with an inscription over the entryway that said: ABANDON ALL HOPE YE WHO ENTER HERE. Dante had it right—the Devil loves to bring despair. If he can bury your hope from the outset, he'll try to put the tombstone of despair over your life. Stand firm though and hold firmly to the promises that God has given. Let those promises take root in your mind each day. Tap into your sixth sense. Remember, you are His child—a new creation!

FURTHER DIAGNOSIS

1. How does a person fall into depression?

2. Why are issues over money and finances often connected to bouts of depression in people?

3. When have you allowed your emotions to dominate your decisions rather than trusting in the promises of God?

4. How can you help someone combat deep despair?

5. How would you describe your identity and hope in God?

FILLING YOUR PRESCRIPTION

1. People who _____ are people who think flourishing thoughts. People who don't flourish have negative and destructive thoughts.

2. _____ is lethal. It can block out the truth of God's infinite love and power, because the person can't see beyond their own personal pain.

3. We should never doubt our ability to switch focus. Learning to _____ your focus produces tremendous rewards in your life.

4. Adjusting your focus when faced with discouraging news is a first line of _____ against the MV of despair overrunning your mind.

5. Jesus's famous story of The Prodigal Son says that the younger brother wasted his life living on the wild side, but then "____ _____ ____ _____ _____".

6. He _____ bought a ticket to a new destination.

7. I used to think that abundance was only _____ for a lucky few. I realized it's available to everyone.

8. _____ is the awareness that you are not defined by your bank account, people's opinions, or the latest gadget.

9. Our minds and emotions often scream that the Bible isn't true and God doesn't really care about us. As those times we have a choice: to depend on our _____and feelings or to trust in God's _____Word.

10. Soon, we learn to recognize the _____ of God like we recognize a dear friends voice.

CHAPTER 7

THE SCIENCE OF THE BRAIN

"What humanity owes to personalities like Buddha, Moses, and Jesus ranks for me higher than all the achievements of the enquiring and constructive mind." — Albert Einstein, Theoretical Physicist, 1879-1955

IN THE MOVIE, *The Wizard of Oz*, the Scarecrow's song has a consistent refrain, "If I only had a brain." Up to that point, he lived in confusion, unable to think, dream, and plan. Before he met Dorothy to take the journey to the Emerald City, the Scarecrow was like any other scarecrow—stuck in a cornfield with no hope for the future. He saw that having a brain was the way to become wise, and his choices on the journey to the Emerald City exercised his mind. He proved to be mindful of his surroundings, words and relationships. He had a brain after all! He began to change when he was freed from his mental hang ups and pointed in a direction to take his first steps.

Over the years, my experience in helping people has often made me aware of their personal mind viruses. Many of the people I've dealt with *want* to have a brain; they *want* to be a thoughtful, caring person, but they seem plagued by MVs that make them, well, brainless.

The story of the Scarecrow made me think about our physical human brain and the connection between it and our emotional and spiritual well-being. I soon became enamored by the study of brain scans. Neurobiologists have studied all kinds of populations. I reviewed brain scans of people with rich prayer lives and those with OCD. I looked at brain scans of homosexuals and lesbians. I look at scans of hardened criminals and other groups of people to discover what is in their brains that makes them do what they do.

After my investigation, I realized that we are pretty much all the same people when we are born—our environment is the primary factor that influences how we think and act. A child doesn't come out of the womb as a racist; he is taught to be racist. A child isn't born wise; she learns to be wise. Other issues are more complex and hotly debated. For instance, I won't settle the issue here of whether LGBTs (Lesbian, Gay, Bisexual and Transgender people) are born that way or if they became LGBT because of events or the environment. There are just as many people who say they were born that way as there are those who say it's a learned behavior. But one thing is for sure: environment plays a major part in shaping our attitudes.

THIS CHAPTER MAY BE A BIT CONTROVERSIAL TO SOME.

As a minister, I believe the most important question isn't, "Were you born that way?" but instead, "Have you been born again?" If you have the Spirit of God communing with your spirit, you can delete mind viruses, you can resist infectious negative thoughts, and you can walk away from a sour mindset.

This chapter may be a bit controversial to some. However, my intent is to reveal the importance of physical and spiritual practices when it comes to defeating mind viruses.

THE BRAIN AND RELIGIOUS PRACTICES

My research led me to the work of two neuroscientists who explain how spirituality affects the brain. In *How God Changes Your Brain*, Dr. Andrew Newberg and Mark Waldman don't claim to be born again believers, but they observe, "If you contemplate God long enough, something surprising happens in the brain. Neural functioning begins to change. Different circuits become activated, while others become deactivated."[10] They spent four years studying different types of people and how their religious practices affected their brains. They have scanned the brains of Buddhists and atheists, and they observed what happens in the brain of Pentecostal people who exercised their gift of speaking in tongues.

Another interesting study is found in *The Amen Solution* by Dr. Daniel G. Amen. He studied the effects of the daily, 12-minute *kirtan kriya* meditation practice. This exercise involves chanting the sounds, *Saa Taa*

---

10. Andrew Newberg, M.D. and Mark Robert Waldman, *How God Changes Your Brain*, Ballantine Books, 2009, p 3.

Naa Maa, while doing repetitive finger movement.[11] It's an interesting practice similar to transcendental meditation, which was popular a few years ago. The main goal of this exercise is to relax the brain and reset your nervous system. While I think this practice is consistent with the proven benefits of mediation, adding faith to the equation takes the practice to another level. Faith enhances expectation, and an expectation that cannot be stopped is an expectation that will not be denied. Newberg and Waldman explain it this way: "If you strongly believe something, if you have faith in yourself, you will stimulate both your immune system and your motivational system into action."[12]

FAITH ENHANCES EXPECTATION, AND AN EXPECTATION THAT CANNOT BE STOPPED IS AN EXPECTATION THAT WILL NOT BE DENIED.

I want to make sure I get the point across: *there is a difference* between meditation alone and meditation combined with faith. Without faith, deep reflections often turn dark and foreboding. The world of psychology describes *rumination* as destructive thinking that is hazardous to mental, relational, and physical health. If you meditate on something frightening or something that stirs anger, you can actually damage your brain. Brain scans in a Stanford study have shown that those who focus on the negative aspects of themselves or a negative interpretation of life had increased activity in a part of the brain called the *amygdala*. In turn, these subjects generated waves of fear and released destructive neurochemicals into the brain. That, of course, is meditation gone wrong. I believe that most meditation is harmless, and may even be helpful at times. Biblical, faith-directed mediation, however, is powerful and productive.

I have been involved with the community of faith for decades. As a pastor, I get to see the full range of human experiences. I have wept with people when they experience excruciating heartaches, and I've rejoiced with those who celebrated the joys of life. I have taught that going to

11. Daniel G. Amen, M.D., *The Amen Solution,* Three Rivers Press, 2011, p 239

12. Andrew Newberg, M.D. and Mark Robert Waldman, *How God Changes Your Brain,* Ballantine Books, 2009, p 34

church and having a daily devotional time with God is the most import-ant thing you can do for self-improvement. Over the years, my wife Kar-en and I have observed the positive effects this has on individuals and families—and the negative effects of neglecting times of connecting with God. Too often, a struggling parent with an adolescent comes to church looking for answers. Some only discover the importance of faith when they begin to notice negative behavior patterns in their child. By then, neural pathways are already established; changing them from negative to positive then requires far more effort, determination, and persistence. It's much more effective if parents start early to expose their kids to the grace and truth of God.

Proverbs 22:6 tells us: "Train up a child in the way they should go and when they are old they will not depart from it." That verse was originally written in ancient Hebrew, and can also be translated: *Train up a child in the way he should go and when whiskers begin to form on the chin they will not depart from it.* When a child needs God in the pivotal time of ado-lescence, the environment they were raised in will affect their decisions with peers, in times of temptation and during trials. A good upbringing, which produces stability and wisdom, will prove to be a treasure.

I remember a very talented young lady in our youth group years ago. She could sing and play an instrument beautifully. When she would share her gift in church, it was obvious that the hand of God was upon her. But she turned away from God at the age of nineteen and went a different direction. Now, twenty-five years later, all of her children and grandchil-dren are struggling with poverty. Once she left the church, she exposed her children to a godless environment, and now her grandchildren have no knowledge of God. From the experience of this woman and her fami-ly, we see that environment affects every aspect of your life.

In Genesis 13, the writer talks about a couple of cities near the Dead Sea that had become so wicked in their thoughts and actions that God decided to destroy them. The actions of the people in Sodom and Go-morrah had veered so far away from morality that perversion instead of righteousness was the norm. God eventually wiped those two cities off the map, and today, scientists believe those towns may have submerged and are part of the Dead Sea.

A righteous man by the name of Lot chose to, *"Pitch his tent near Sodom"* (Genesis 13:12). Each day when he opened his tent flap, the first thing Lot saw was his neighbors wallowing in perversion, and it tormented him.

Foolishly, he raised two daughters in this environment. An angel gave Lot an early alert warning to get out of Sodom because God was about to rain down fire upon it. He fled to the hills with his wife and two girls, just in the nick of time before the twin cities were annihilated.

However, the years living the shadow of Sodom and Gomorrah's evil, envy and cruelty affected the minds and the morality of Lot and his family. Even after they fled the destruction of the cities, they suffered from poor choices. Lot's wife died that day due to an act of disobedience. She was turned into a pillar of salt because she was too proud to follow the admonition and instruction of the Lord. Later, Lot was alone with his two daughters in the mountains. Lot's daughters got their father drunk and committed incest with him. Unthinkable, you say? Their actions were the result of the environment where they were raised and influenced.

ACTIONS ARE A RESULT OF ENVIRONMENT.

Wisdom, maturity, and godliness don't come by accident or by magic. They become part of the life of a growing child only when parents take time to invest spiritual concepts in their children. In the times of the Bible, the religious people had some unusual spiritual disciplines. When a child was a baby, the parents would dip their fingers in honey, touch the first word of the Torah (Moses' Bible), and then touch it to the lips of the newborn baby, praying that the words of Moses would become sweet to the child. Devout Jewish families would make sure their children had memorized all (or at least most) of the five books of Moses. The practice was helped the child understand the importance of the Word of God.

Recently, I listened to a young man sing in our church. He was incredible! He brought the crowd to a standing ovation. I know the history of that man. He is the victim of abuse that devastated him. In many cases, people never recover from the damage inflicted through this kind of cruelty, but this young man is obviously making great strides in rejecting the mind viruses of shame, rage, and fear. He is replacing them with the wonder of God's love, grace, truth, and sovereign power. I wish everyone responded like this young man. I have the greatest admiration for abuse victims who find the courage to find healing and hope in the grace of God.

As a pastor, I plead with parents to make sure they expose their children to corporate worship experiences, but there are no guarantees of the immediate impact. I have a pastor friend who has two boys who were raised in church. They regularly heard the message of the gospel of grace, but when they were older, the boys told their dad his messages were antiquated and irrelevant. Their attitudes looked hopeless, but the seed of truth had been planted in their minds. When a visiting speaker went to their church, it was a game-changer for these two young men. The speaker had the gift of an evangelist (see Ephesians 4 for the five-fold ministry of the church), and his message made such an impact on those boys that both of them were called into full-time ministry. They came back to the biblical roots of their childhood. God used the evangelist's words to change the trajectory of the lives of these two young men. The resources used by the Spirit of God were the long, patient investments of love and truth by their parents.

What does going to church do for the brain? As a pastor, I often see the value of raising children in a church so they encounter positive spiritual influences. Of course, not all church experiences are positive. I've talked to men and women who felt deeply hurt by churches that seemed to be more interested in following man-made rules than loving and obeying Jesus Christ. If you don't have a church, I highly suggest that you find a Spirit-filled one where the Bible is the number one textbook and the people are exuberant in their worship.

NEGLECTING THE COMMUNITY OF BELIEVERS WILL ALWAYS RESULT IN SPIRITUAL AND RELATIONAL PROBLEMS.

I believe in the value of a Spirit-filled worship service. Many churches only deal with the letter of the law and not the Spirit. If you raise children in a church where there is too much "letter of the law," they eventually will *dry up* and find church boring and judgmental. However, if you find a church that is "all Spirit" and little Word, you and your kids may *blow up* in emotionalism. But if you can find a good Bible-based, Spirit-filled congregation, you will *grow up*.

As a reaction against the perceived strict moralism, harsh legalism, and irrelevant messages of the church, a number of people have decided to avoid church. They assume they can be "good Christians" on their own. The Bible never envisions the people of God being isolated. We grow only in community, and we can't duplicate what happens when God's people get together. The writer of Hebrews says it this way: "Let us not neglect our meeting together, as some people do." (Hebrews 10:25 *NLT*). Neglecting the community of believers will always result in spiritual and relational problems. We pay a high price for the pride of thinking we don't need to follow God's directions to engage in meaningful interactions and corporate worship. And our children will suffer, too.

A church certainly can be destructive if leaders describe an angry, authoritarian God who fills you with fear and motivates you with threats. Religion, in its worst form, controls every aspect of life, exploits the weak, and heaps on people man-made rules that strangle creativity. Colossians 2 tells us:

> Since you died with Christ to the elemental spiritual forces of this world, why, as though you still belonged to the world, do you submit to its rules: "Do not handle! Do not taste! Do not touch!"? These rules, which have to do with things that are all destined to perish with use, are based on merely human commands and teachings. Such regulations indeed have an appearance of wisdom, with their self-imposed worship, their false humility and their harsh treatment of the body, but they lack any value in restraining sensual indulgence. (Colossians 2:20-23 *NIV*).

Godly obedience is always motivated by the wonder of God's grace and the wisdom of God's directions in our lives.

I am a strong proponent for education, but education in and of itself isn't enough. If information could save us, then the Internet would have saved us because it's a torrent of knowledge spewing out each day. We need to expose people to events and people so something in their brains can be triggered, and consequently, move them into a greater level of spiritual perception and practice. What can do something so positive? The powerful combination of God's truth, God's Spirit, and God's people.

THE SCIENCE OF THE BRAIN

Before I explain why the way we connect and perceive God is so important, let me give you a lesson in Neuroscience 101. Newberg and Waldman explain a simple way to envision the important parts of our brain:

> First, put two imaginary almonds (without the shells) in the palm of your hand. These are the two halves of your amygdala, which governs your fight-or-flight response to a perceived or imagined fear. Next, place two halves of an imaginary walnut (again, no shell) into the palm of your hand. This is your thalamus, which sends sensory

information to all the other parts of the brain. It also gives you a sense of meaning, and what reality may actually be.

Now, make a fist and bend your forearm so your knuckles are pointing to the ceiling. Your forearm is your spinal cord, and your fist (along with the almond halves and the walnut) is the limbic system, the oldest part of the brain that every reptile, fish, amphibian, bird, and mammal has. Your limbic system is involved with memory encoding, emotional response, and many other bodily functions.

Next, take four sheets of eight-by-ten-inch paper and place them on top of your fist. Crumple the paper up so it fits snugly, and voila!–you have a human brain. Those four sheets of paper are the approximate size and thickness of your neocortex, and all the memories, beliefs and behaviors you have learned over a lifetime are stored on them, along with all of your visual, auditory, motor, language, and cognitive processing centers of the brain. Thirty percent of that paper is your frontal lobe, which sits directly behind and above your eyes. It controls nearly everything you are conscious of: your logic, reason, attention, language skills, and voluntary motivation.

Notice where the crumpled paper touches your thumb. That area approximates the location of the anterior cingulate, which processes social awareness, intuition, and empathy. It also contains a unique type of neuron that only humans and a few primates have. There's one more area that I want you to keep in mind: your parietal lobes, located above and slightly behind your ears. They take up less than a quarter of those sheets of paper, but provide you with a sense of yourself in relation to other objects in the world. When activity in this area decreases, you can feel at one with God, the universe, or any other concept you are consciously focusing on.[13]

This is a lot to grasp; however, the point is that our God created in each of us an incredible computer—the human mind. As we meditate, study and pray, it alters the function of each of the parts of our brain!

Dr. Newberg identifies God Circuits which are built into our brain. From early childhood, God exists in every person's brain as a combination of ideas, images, feelings, sensations, and relationships. The key neural structures and circuits that shape our perception of God look like this:

---

13. Andrew Newberg, M.D. and Mark Robert Waldman, *How God Changes Your Brain*, Ballantine Books, 2009, p 16-17

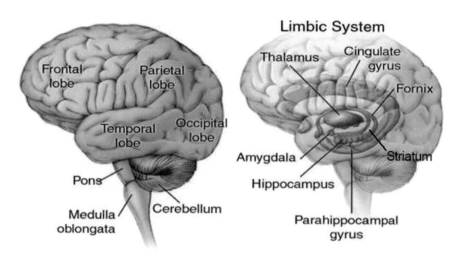

Anatomy of the Brain

OCCIPITAL-PARIETAL CIRCUIT

Identifies God as an object that exists in the world. Young children see God as a face because their brains cannot process abstract spiritual concepts.

PARIETAL-FRONTAL CIRCUIT

Establishes a relationship between the two objects known as "you" and "God." It places God in space and allows you to experience God's presence. If you increase activity in your parietal lobe through meditation or intense prayer, the boundaries between you and God dissolve. You feel a sense of unity with the object of contemplation and your spiritual beliefs.

FRONTAL LOBE

Creates and integrates all of your ideas about God positive or negative— including the logic you use to evaluate your religious and spiritual beliefs. It predicts your future in relationship to God and attempts to intellectually answer the "why, what, and where" questions raised by spiritual issues.

THALAMUS

Gives emotional meaning to your concepts of God. The thalamus gives you a holistic sense of the world and appears to be the key organ that makes God feel objectively real.

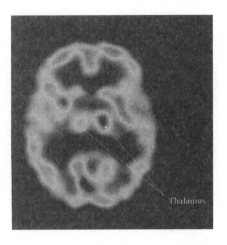

AMYGDALA

When overly stimulated, the amygdala creates the emotional impression of a frightening, authoritative, and punitive God, and it suppresses the frontal lobe's ability to logically think about God.

STRIATUM

Inhibits activity in the amygdala, allowing you to feel safe in the presence of God, or of whatever object or concept you are contemplating.

ANTERIOR CINGULATE

Allows you to experience God as loving and compassionate. It decreases religious anxiety, guilt, fear, and anger by suppressing activity in the amygdala.[14]

Let's examine the thalamus, the part of the brain that helps us identify what is and what isn't real. It also gives us the sense of emotional meaning to our thoughts. When Newberg and Waldman conducted their studies, they found that the more a person meditated on a specific object—like God—the thalamus became more active, until a point was reached where thoughts were perceived in the same way other senses were perceived. In other words, the more you meditate on God, the more God will be sensed by your brain as real, and you will ultimately feel closer to Him.

---

14. Andrew Newberg, M.D. and Mark Robert Waldman, *How God Changes Your Brain*, Ballantine Books, 2009, p 43-44, fig.p 54

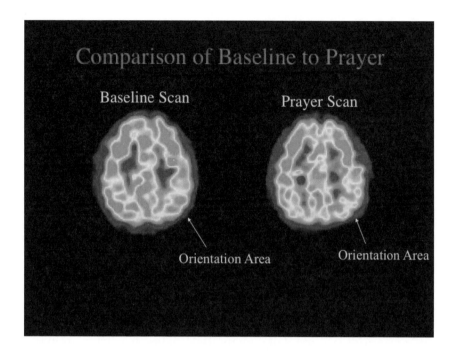

This is a scan of a person who has meditated and prayed for more than fifteen years, and her thalamus is irregular. The asymmetry (irregularity) in the scan shows that the person is experiencing more than thought; she actually feels what she is thinking about. The thalamus doesn't distinguish the difference between our psychological emotions (like hurt, fear, anger, joy, love, and gratitude) and what we can physically feel with our hands (pain and pleasure). For a person who practices prayer, faith becomes neurologically real—felt, thought, and experienced.

Other studies have shown that when a person speaks in tongues, there is more brain activity in the parietal lobe. Dr. Newberg reported: "This gives them the sense that a separate entity is communicating with them."[15]

God has made every area of our brain to experience Him. Researchers tell us that when we pray quietly, it affects certain parts of the brain, while praying out loud effects another part of the brain. I often pray silently, and I also pray out loud. I have done this for decades. Also, I have received the gift of speaking in tongues and use this gift on a daily basis.

---

15. Andrew Newberg, M.D. and Mark Robert Waldman, *How God Changes Your Brain,* Ballantine Books, 2009, p 52

Newberg and Waldman discovered that people who spoke in tongues showed remarkable changes in brain scans. (Please keep in mind that the Bible term for speaking in tongues is *Glossolalia*.) This is their finding:

"Instead of focusing one's attention on a specific phrase or ideal, which increases activity in the frontal lobe, the practitioner surrenders voluntary control and thus a significant degree of ordinary consciousness—by deliberately slowing down frontal lobe activity. This, in turn, allows the limbic areas of the brain to become more active, which neurologically increases the emotional intensity of the experience. With the nuns and Buddhists, the opposite experience occurs. Frontal lobe activity increases, limbic activity decreases, and the combination generates a peaceful and serene state of consciousness. Interestingly, both the nuns and Pentecostalists felt that our study demonstrated that God could intervene and directly influence the brain."[16]

The scan (below) shows more activity in the parietal lobe during prayer than when at rest. And remember, the parietal lobe is the part of our brain where relationships are established. Being a person who prays for extended periods of time daily, I can attest that this is true—praying to God strengthens my relationships! When I first became a born-again believer, my prayer time wasn't as deep and strong as it is now. Over the years, the more time I spend listening to God, talking to Him, and speaking in tongues has drawn me closer Him. I can sense how very real He is in my life.

God, in His infinite wisdom, constructed our brains in a way that enhance our relationship with Him. Until we see Him in glory, we can't observe Him with our physical eyes, but our brain is able to register that He is with us. The limbic system (which happens to be the oldest part of our brain) helps us create an emotional and meaningful experience of God, while the frontal lobe (which is the newest part of our brain) helps us have a view of God that is sensible, thoughtful and loving. Put those two balanced brain activities together, and we have a positive experience of God.

One of the most interesting findings the studies of the effects of prayer on the brain is that the experience is unique to each individual. Different parts of the brain are affected to different degrees for each person. In light of this, 1 Corinthians 12:11 takes on a greater meaning: "But one and the

---

16. Andrew Newberg, M.D. and Mark Robert Waldman, *How God Changes Your Brain,* Ballantine Books, 2009, p 49, fig. p 51

same Spirit works all these things, distributing to each one individually just as He wills." Our God communicates with us individually!

NO BRAIN PAIN, NO SANE GAIN

Just like every other part of our body, our brain needs a regular workout. Here is the countdown of eight ways to keep your mind mentally active. I extracted the following practices on mental health from Newberg and Waldman, and have paraphrased their material for you. Keep in mind these guys are not particularly born-again believers. Yet take note of what they have found to be the number one contributor to a healthy brain:

Number Eight: *Smile*

Sounds simple enough doesn't it. However, if you look at the people around you, whether you are in an office, a subway, bus or supermarket, what do you see? People who appear to be sad, stressed, and lonely. Do they really feel that way? Unless we know the personal circumstances of every person, we can only read the expressions on their faces, which generally is not a smile. The old phrase, "Turn that frown upside down" takes on new meaning. Putting a smile on our faces makes the nerves in our brain stronger so we can maintain a more positive outlook on life. Even if you have to fake it – smile! People around you will respond better, and pretty soon, the smile will be genuine.

Number Seven: *Stay Intellectually Active*

Make time every day to read, solve math problems, play word games, watch education and science channels on TV—anything that will stimulate your brain. When you engage in these activities, you strengthen your brain and reduce your chances of getting angry or fearful. Research has further shown that when you read the Bible and reflect on what you've read (or discuss it with others), complex circuits in your brain are activated. Be smarter . . . read your Bible!

Number Six: *Relax Your Brain*

Simple, repetitive activities that bring you happiness and are meaningful are an effective way to relax your brain. Listen to pleasant music while taking some deep breaths—or maybe you enjoy knitting or crocheting, or saying The Lord's Prayer or The Prayer of Jabez over and over. Familiar and repetitive activities will relax you.

Number Five: *Yawn*

Studies have shown that when you yawn, you stimulate neural activity in the part of the brain that creates feelings of empathy. Yawning is very important to the function of your brain, but over the years, it has been interpreted as physical exhaustion or boredom with the people around us. It's true that the more tired you are, the more prone you are to yawn, but the benefits of yawning are receiving more recognition as a way to intensify reasoning and awareness. Try this, the next time you're in a meeting and everyone is looking like they're having a hard time staying away—take a 30-second yawn break! Encourage everyone to yawn, and participation in your meeting will take on new life.

Number Four: *Meditate/Pray*

If you meditate or pray for 20 to 60 minutes, your physical and emotional health will improve. I know a lot of us don't always have that much time during the day to devote to meditation, but studies have shown that even ten to fifteen minutes of prayer or meditation have an affect on our mental health.

Number Three: *Aerobic Exercise*

For years we have heard health experts recommend enough exercise to become physically tired to counter mental tiredness. Intense exercise has been shown to help our minds as well as our bodies get into shape. The key is to just start exercising and remain consistent. Don't try to run five miles the first day. First try walking short distances. Begin at an easy, attainable, sustainable level, but *start moving and remain consistent!*

Number Two: *Talk With Others*

We were created to have meaningful social interaction. The Bible tells us this was God's plan: "Then the Lord God said, 'It is not good for the man to be alone. I will make a helper who is just right for him'" (Genesis 2:18 *NLT*). God, in His great wisdom, knew that we need someone to talk to, and created us so that our brains benefit from conversations. However, when you just talk about the weather or other trivial matters, your brain doesn't engage as much as when you talk about more important things, such as God's purposes, resolving conflict, helping the poor, and resolving community problems. Be careful that those conversations don't escalate to angry discussions, which cause damage to your brain.

Number One: Faith

Faith is the number one factor that stimulates optimism. I say this every week as people exit our services: "Go away with high expectations that 'if God be for us who can be against us!'" When you exercise faith, it combats the doubt and fear that arise from the limbic system, and the supernatural begins to unfold in your life. Your expectations should and do rise. In turn, the whole brain becomes brilliantly alive. The longer you are filled with faith, the more you change the neural circuitry of your brain.[17] "Focus on God long enough, and God becomes neurologically real."[18]

BOTTOM LINE IS THIS

We were all born into sin. Since Adam and Eve chose to disobey God, we've all suffered. When we were born, we were born in sin (John 9:34), and the enemy uses evil and sin to kill, steal and destroy our lives.

I have some attitudes and behaviors that I don't particularly like. I don't know where they came from, but they nag me like a pesky fly. I wonder who in my family tree allowed this Mind Virus to take hold of them and were never able to shed it. I tend to be judgmental. I don't know why, and I sure don't spend all day thinking about how I'm delighted to be judgmental. As a matter of fact, I've lived so long that I can immediately catch myself when a judgmental Mind Virus is trying to take hold.

I've gone to God on many occasions like a sick person would go to a doctor for a remedy—and He is always faithful and gives me the same prescription that I have been using for decades: prayer, praise and the Scriptures. Whenever I have the tendency to want to judge another person, I begin to pray blessing on them. It works every time. I dispel a Mind Virus by spiritual disciplines.

If you're a serious student of the Bible, you know that in Acts 2:42-47 the church is at the apex of harmony and happiness. People were getting along like they really liked each other. How did they do that? Watch this:

That day about three thousand took him at his word, were baptized and were signed up. They committed themselves to the teaching of the apostles, the life together, the common meal, and the prayers.

Everyone around was in awe—all those wonders and signs done through the apostles! And all the believers lived in a wonderful

---

17. Andrew Newberg, M.D. and Mark Robert Waldman, *How God Changes Your Brain,* Ballantine Books, 2009, pgs 149-165

18. Ibid., p 165

harmony, holding everything in common. They sold whatever they owned and pooled their resources so that each person's need was met.

They followed a daily discipline of worship in the Temple followed by meals at home, every meal a celebration, exuberant and joyful, as they praised God. People in general liked what they saw. Every day their number grew as God added those who were saved. (Acts 2:42-47 The Message)

Did you notice how happy people were? And did you notice what brought about such harmony? It was the result of their daily discipline of worship in the Temple combined with exuberant fellowship with believers. Earlier in the passage, we see that they gave themselves to the teaching of the apostles, life together, the common meal and prayers. Worship, food and fellowship—it has always been a recipe for spiritual growth.

A young surgeon and I were having a meal recently. He has had some life changing experiences that are bringing him closer to God. He is a highly intelligent man, but he sometimes struggles to make worship meaningful and express himself to God. He excused his difficulties as, "That's just the way I am." Still, he didn't give up on the disciplines. He committed himself to read through the Old Testament and serious prayer. Then it happened—while in church one day, he felt a tremendous desire to dance before the Lord, even though that is not a regular practice at our church. You have to remember, this is a surgeon. I asked him, "How did you change your mind on worship?"

He replied, "It was the Old Testament and praying." Getting into the Bible and spending time meditating changed a Mind Virus that had infected him for quite some time.

God designed every detail of our brain so we could get to know Him better and communicate with Him. There is a bridge, a link, a connection between the physical brain, our emotions, our reasoning, and our spiritual wellbeing. God has given us excellent methods and effective practices to integrate into our spiritual lifestyle. We'll take a look at them in the next few chapters.

FURTHER DIAGNOSIS

1. List the factors (past and present) that affect the development of your brain. What are the most influential factors?

2. Looking back at your life, what positive and/or negative experiences affected your perception of yourself, your future, and God?

3. If you're currently employed or have had a job in the past, how has your workplace environment affected your sense of identity and your outlook on life?

4. What has God shown you in prayer recently that has affected your mindset toward others?

5. Why are the physical aspects of the brain important to understand if we are creatures made with a spirit?

FILLING YOUR PRESCRIPTION

1. _____ plays a major part in shaping our attitude.

2. There is a difference between meditation _____ and meditation combined with _____.

3. Lot's daughter got her father drunk and committed incest with him. Their actions were the result of the environment where they were _____ and _____.

4. I have the greatest admiration for abuse victims who find the _____ to find healing and hope in the grace of God.

5. If information could save us, then the _____ would have saved us.

6. The more you meditate on God, the more God will be _____ by your brain as real, and you will ultimately feel closer to Him.

7. God has made every area of your brain to _____ Him.

8. Just like every other part of our body, our brain needs a _____ workout.

9. Faith is the number one factor that stimulates _____.

10. Whenever I have the tendency to want to _____ another person, I begin to _____ blessings over them. It works every time. I dispel a Mind Virus by spiritual disciplines.

CHAPTER 8

RENEWING YOUR MIND

"I consider wisdom supernatural because it isn't taught by men— it's a gift from God." — Joyce Meyer, American Christian Author, 1943-

GOOD HYGIENE—preserving your health through the practice of cleanliness—involves a good deal of time by being conscious of washing your hands, taking showers, and using hot water to combat the worst bugs. Whether filling up the car at the gas station, shopping at the supermarket, going to a movie, eating at a restaurant or a community event, it always seems that sanitized hand wipes, anti-bacterial gels, soaps and disposal towels are everywhere. If you want to stay healthy, you become very conscious of what other people touch and use. You make every effort to kill the cold and flu bugs that linger in public areas. Well, spiritual hygiene—renewing and preserving your mind's health in God—involves the same vigilance.

In the Bible, the Apostle Paul's letter to the Romans involves a lot of heavenly hygiene practices and warnings. The book is considered one of the most brilliant pieces of literature ever written. He clearly and boldly articulates a wide range of truths, including the nature of God, sin, redemption, faith, grace, creation, Christian hope, spiritual life, relationships, the duties of citizenship, ethics, forgiveness, and many more. In the first 11 chapters, Paul lays out his principles and theology. Then, as he begins the next chapter, he turns his attention to practical application. The hinge passage that connects both parts is in the opening verses:

> I beseech you therefore, brethren, by the mercies of God, that you present your bodies a living sacrifice, holy, acceptable to God, which is your reasonable service. And do not be conformed to this world, but be transformed by the renewing of your mind, that you may prove

what is that good and acceptable and perfect will of God. (Romans 12:1-2, *NKJV*).

An important instruction that changed my life is Paul's exhortation: stop conforming to the world's ways; be transformed. How? By renewing your mind. If you split the word "conformed" into two parts, you discover a hidden truth. *Con* is the prefix that we attach to words like "convict", "constrict" and "conceal". It means "with." In the middle of the word is *formed* which means structure and substance. Paul tells us to avoid being connected to our old form of life any longer. The old form of life may be activities and habits, but it also includes the values and presuppositions underneath the behaviors—the unseen world of the heart. We often think of ourselves as a physical body with a soul, but we're a spirit that happens to live in a physical body. Transformation is the ability to rise above or change from an existing form to another, and renewing our minds each day—a spiritual wash to refresh and strengthen—is a habit to embrace.

Let's do another word study in the passage. Take the word *transformed* and split it. The prefix "trans" means "across", "beyond" or "through". We use this prefix for words such as "transcend", "transport" or "transfix". The word *formed* again means structure or substance. Paul is trying to get us to see something wonderful here. Can you see it?

GOD WANTS TO CHANGE THE SUBSTANCE OF OUR LIVES.

We aren't meant to stay stuck in the same old way of life. God wants to *change the substance of our lives.* We are radically transformed only when our minds are renewed according to the Word of God. This doesn't happen in our physical bodies. Our physical existence isn't what makes us unique and special in the eyes of God. A biologist observed that everything you find in a human body could also be found in a pig. Isn't that's comforting? Our souls make us unique in all creation.

When you live exclusively by the physical world, you experience significant limitations. Think about those limits for a moment. You can only lift so much weight, you can only run so fast, and you can only work so hard. These limitations involve the body, but limitations in the spiritual world are truly troublesome. If something inside your spirit is crippling your capacity to dream and do what is right—something destructive is truly at work.

STAY HEALTHY—DEFY YOUR FIVE SENSES

As a Christian, I exist in two worlds: material and immaterial. In order to avoid being limited by the material world, I must live in a way that defies my five senses. I've placed my five senses in a lockbox so they don't dominate my spiritual life. Paul had the same perspective. In describing the call of Abraham as the father of faith, Paul told the Romans that God is the One "who gives life to the dead and calls into being things that were not" (Romans 4:17). The "things that are not" are the things in the spiritual, immaterial world. Paul says it's important to acknowledge their existence.

The five senses are the way we navigate the material world, but they are severely limited in helping us relate to the spiritual world. We see God's majesty in creation, and we feel the loving touch of family and friends. These realities, though, point to a spiritual universe that can't be seen, but it's even *more real* that everything we see, taste, touch, smell and hear.

To know God and grow in our faith, we have to learn to operate in the spiritual world. We have to avoid letting the physical world—and all the messages, hopes, and promises of this world—squeeze us into its mold. Instead, God wants to squeeze us into His mold so we look, sound, and act more like Jesus. When we find Him to be more wonderful than any treasure the earth promises, God takes an average life and transforms it into an extraordinary life! I call it "finding the jet stream of God." Just like an airplane finds the jet stream in the sky and flies higher and faster, you can experience God's best by living in the Spirit.

If you're confused by the term *living in the Spirit,* think of it as living in the realm of a sixth sense. It's another connection, a sixth ability to be in touch with reality—but this is about *spiritual* reality. This connection is the most important thing in a person's life—more valuable than gold, and worth more than all the diamonds, furs and real estate on the planet! Let me ask you a question: If you could have any miracle, what would you ask for? Would you like a billion dollars? Most of us believe that money will make us happy. Otherwise, people wouldn't spend billions on the lottery every week. A billion dollars can make you happy (at least for a while), but you would still be limited by your five senses.

The most valuable thing we can have is a sharp awareness of spiritual realities. If I only live by my five senses, I'm impoverished! Unfortunately, most people (even many Christians) never even try to develop their sixth sense of spiritual perception. They have their five senses, but their spiritual bank accounts are empty. Tapping into the Spirit not only makes miracles possible––it makes them commonplace. It far better than having a billion dollars in the bank! You have access to the divine power of the universe. You're no longer limited by your five senses.

TAPPING INTO THE SPIRIT NOT ONLY MAKES MIRACLES POSSIBLE—IT MAKES THEM COMMONPLACE.

Another way to think about spiritual life is location: *local versus non-local*. If you grow up in one place all of your life, you're only familiar and comfortable with the local streets, buildings, and people. If you don't travel to other places in the country and the world, your cultural experience becomes severely limited. You have to go non-local—outside the range of everyday resources and experience to find something unusual and rare.

Karen and I live in a desert climate in Central California that has unique resources, experiences and foods in that region. However, if we want cool weather in August, we have to go to the coast. If we want certain foods, we have to go to grocery stores that sell products from all over the world or go to restaurants that serve exotic cuisine. For example, you'd be hard pressed to find anyone in Central California who has eaten (or can spell) *sopapilla*. Yet, if I want sopapilla for dessert, I need to go to Texas. To get there, I have to go beyond the limitations of my location, board a plane for Texas, and land in one of the cities there. My yearning for something better and beyond what I can experience locally is what sparks my desire to travel. Our yearnings fuel the change of where we go and what we do. In order to tap into a limitless supply of inspiration, you have to long for something higher and better than what you have experienced already.

Your spirit is capable of giving you information and connections far beyond your natural abilities. A whole world of spiritual realities is out there waiting for you! Don't get in the habit of violating your spiritual thirst. That's violating your Early Alert System (EAS) of inner, God-prompted desires. Learn to trust your EAS—it's your connection to God. Continue to violate the EAS and soon you'll be acting like everyone else, conforming to the world's values and habits and limited by your five senses.

GOD'S NUDGE

Many people think connecting with the supernatural world is spooky, but it's entirely normal for people who are in tune with spiritual reality. Most of the time, people call these experiences "coincidences." They happen, but we can't explain how or why. For example, you were thinking of a family member or friend, and then you received an unexpected phone call from her. A coincidence? Possibly, but it may be a spiritual connection that can't be seen or measured.

How can a mother sit in a room and know a baby is crying in another room? She didn't hear a sound, but somehow, she knows. She tells her husband, "You'd better go check on the baby. She's crying."

The husband looks at her with a funny expression and replies, "I don't hear a thing."

He's trusting in his sense of hearing, but she has a deeper, stronger, spiritual connection with her baby. How does she know about her child? Many mothers have a sixth sense, a spiritual connection with their children. How can we develop this kind of perception?

Like any other gift, talent or skill, our sixth sense needs to be carefully developed. Some Christians have a spiritual gift (some call it "discernment") to be able to detect the presence of the supernatural around them. But all believers have this capacity to some degree. For example, I know some people who have the uncanny ability to know something is wrong in a friend's life, even if they haven't talked in months and the friend lives across the country. That's a gift! All of us, however, can develop a deeper level of spiritual sensitivity. We can pick up on spiritual cues and sense the nudges of God, and then respond in obedience and faith. That ability isn't limited to the super-spiritual saints; it's standard operating procedure for every child of God.[19]

GOD'S CLEANSING AGENT: THE WORD

The most spiritually enlightened people usually practice some form of daily meditation. When we become aware of MVs and the need to keep our minds fresh, clean, and bursting with creative and constructive thoughts, we follow

---

19. To find out more about recognizing and responding to spiritual promptings, read my book, *The God Nudge*. You'll find out how to order it by looking at the resources page in the back of this book.

up with the focus to concentrate on things noble and good. That focus is rewarded with making friends who are wise and noble in mind and heart, but also in the studying of God's Word. When we meditate and dwell on that Word, our actions and habits begin to change. When our actions and habits begin to change, we are setting a new course for life.

> **WHEN OUR ACTIONS AND HABITS BEGIN TO CHANGE, WE ARE SETTING A NEW COURSE FOR LIFE.**

Meditation is a critical component in our transformation. When you spend time meditating, you engage the spiritual world. I love the Old Testament prophet Isaiah. He had a sharp sense that God's mind and heart are far beyond the physical senses. He wrote, "For My thoughts are not your thoughts, neither are your ways My ways, declares the Lord. As the heavens are higher than the earth, so are My ways higher than your ways and My thoughts than your thoughts" (Isaiah 55:8-9).

This Scripture says my thoughts are limited in comparison to God's thoughts. He has thoughts that I don't have and will never have. After all, He's infinite, and I'm finite—but God still invites me to draw close and listen. His thoughts are wondrous. I won't grasp the fullness of His mind and heart until I meet Him face to face, but when I'm intimately connected to Him I will grasp far more spiritually here on Earth than I ever could through my own strength. How do I tap into the higher thoughts of God? I've spent my life pursuing God's mind and heart, and I'm convinced anyone can. Some of my friends tell me they could never have that kind of intimate, powerful relationship with God, but I disagree. I believe God is longing to speak to every one of us. The prophet Hanani told King Asa in 2 Chronicles 16:9 (and I am paraphrasing here) that God's eyes range throughout the earth seeking for someone He can share His thoughts with. He's still looking for people to share His heart with. I'm one of them. Are you?

JESUS AND THE PARANORMAL

We often think of the word "paranormal" as quirky and amusing, but it's a perfectly legitimate concept to describe a rich, vibrant, intimate connection with the spiritual world. The word means "not scientifically

RENEWING YOUR MIND   129

explainable; supernatural."[20] In many ways, this kind of connection with God is the polar opposite of a mind virus. It's more like the red blood cells that carry life-giving oxygen and nutrients to every part of our bodies, and it's like white blood cells that fight off invading bacteria and viruses. A rich, intimate relationship with the God of the universe is available for every believer. On the night Jesus was betrayed—after dinner but before His arrest—He took His men to the hills outside Jerusalem to give them some final instructions. Jesus explained that He was going to be leaving them, but He was sending them the Holy Spirit of God. No, they wouldn't be able to see the Spirit, but it would be an even better arrangement. The Holy Spirit would live inside them! Jesus words that night must have blown their minds. He explained,

> I tell you the truth, anyone who believes in Me will do the same works I have done, and even greater works, because I am going to be with the Father. And I will ask the Father, and He will give you another Advocate, who will never leave you. He is the Holy Spirit, who leads into all truth. The world cannot receive Him, because it isn't looking for Him and doesn't recognize Him. But you know Him, because He lives with you now and later will be in you (John 14:12,16-17, NLT).

In Jesus' life, we get many glimpses of what this kind of spiritual perception looks like. Luke tells us about an event that took place at a dinner in a Pharisee's house. At the time, Jesus was very popular, and Simon the Pharisee invited the new celebrity and His entourage to his house. It was a status thing for Simon, but things went terribly wrong. In the middle of the dinner, a prostitute barged into the dining room. As everyone looked on, she poured perfume on Jesus' feet, wept tears of joy, and wiped His feet with her hair. Simon was outraged! Luke takes us into the scene: "When the Pharisee who asked Jesus to come to his house saw this, he thought to himself, 'If Jesus were a prophet, He would know that the woman touching Him is a sinner!' " (Luke 7:39 NCV).

The Pharisees prided themselves on being morally pure and physically distant from "undesirable elements" in their communities, so this prostitute's presence was unbearable. It didn't matter to him that this woman had undoubtedly met Jesus at some point before this dinner and had experienced the depths of His love and forgiveness. She had come to Simon's house not to show disrespect to him, but to pour out her love to Jesus.

---

20. "paranormal." Merriam-Webster.com. 2014. Accessed on November 3, 2014. http://www.merriam-webster.com/dictionary/paranormal

Instead, Simon blamed Jesus for not being outraged at the intrusion. Simon completely missed the point involving Jesus' love for outcasts and sinners, and the woman's response of unbridled gratitude. Simon mumbled to himself: "If Jesus were a prophet, he would know that the woman touching him is a sinner!"

Jesus knew what Simon was thinking and asked questions that exposed the Pharisee's hypocrisy. Jesus pointed out that Simon hadn't even given the dusty preacher the common courtesies offered to any guest, but the woman had extravagantly expressed her devotion to Him from the moment she entered the room. This was an important moment to teach everyone present at the dinner (and those who read about it now) about the difference between a hard heart and a tender, grateful heart. The point, though, was made clear only because Jesus sensed what was going on in Simon's mind. Our sixth sense, our spiritual sensitivity can perceive what is going in the mind of a person, but only when we have plenty of practice and humility. How can we be capable of doing the same thing? Jesus was talking to His disciples one day and told them: "He who believes in Me, the works that I do he will do also, and greater works than these he will do because I go to My Father" (John 14:12, *NKJV*).

Again and again in the gospels, we read that Jesus had an uncanny understanding of human nature. He could sense the particular thoughts of the people around Him. John tells us that Jesus' sixth sense was finely tuned and highly developed. Early in his gospel, John explains, "for He knew all men, and because He did not need anyone to testify concerning man, for He Himself knew what was in man" (John 2:24-25, *NASB*).

THE POWER OF THE SPIRIT IS AVAILABLE TO US—IF WE'LL ONLY GET ON GOD'S AGENDA.

Jesus wasn't limited by time and space. Mark paints a picture of a moment when a mother asked Jesus to cast a demon out of her daughter. After a short conversation with the woman, Jesus told her to go home. He explained that the mom's faith was enough: The demon had left her daughter. How did He do that? It was long-distance deliverance. The mother arrived at home, found her daughter, and discovered the demon was gone. As God's children and ambassadors, the power of the Spirit is available to us—if we'll only get on God's agenda, care about His Kingdom, and trust Him to have us do greater works because the Holy Spirit is living in us.

HEAVENLY CONNECTIONS

Some connections are easy to believe because we can see them. If a pickup needs to be pulled to an auto shop, we connect it with another pickup by using a chain or braided rope between them. If a car won't start because the battery is low, we connect jumper cables and it starts up right away. There's nothing supernatural about such connections because they are simply two points connected in the physical world.

There are, of course, some connections that remain invisible to the naked eye that we count on each day. When I flip on a light switch, I don't see electricity coursing into my home through the wires and into the bulb—but it's real. Today, microwaves make cell phone connections. Our smart phones open up the world of the Internet while we're walking or driving. Millions of people are wirelessly connected. Of course, these connections are not visible, but we use them all the time and often take such connections for granted. The entire physical world is based on the validity of points of connection. When connections operate well, good things take place. When connections fail, messages fail to arrive on time, people get frustrated, and businesses lose profit.

Spiritual connections are not visible to the eye, but they are even more real than a wireless connection. In one of Paul's letters to the Corinthians, he wanted to encourage them that the suffering they were currently experiencing wasn't the full story. He reminded them there's an unseen spiritual world full of hope and promises. He wrote,

> For our present troubles are small and won't last very long. Yet they produce for us a glory that vastly outweighs them and will last forever! So we don't look at the troubles we can see now; rather, we fix our gaze on things that cannot be seen. For the things we see now will soon be gone, but the things we cannot see will last forever (2 Corinthians 4:17-18 NLT).

One of the most important tasks for every believer is to train our minds and hearts to be in touch with the spiritual world. If we only see what's going on in the tangible, physical world, we'll be deeply discouraged by heartaches. We'll lose perspective on God's purposes for the blessings we enjoy. We need to put on our spiritual glasses so we can clearly see Kingdom realities. Sooner or later, our new, richer, deeper perceptions become second nature. We sense spiritual realities by being immersed in the Bible and filled with the Spirit. All spiritual hygiene begins with the Scripture and God's Spirit challenging and comforting us to do what is right and good.

Many people are confused about God's purpose and direction for them. The number one question people ask me is "What's God's will for my life?" One of the most important principles is that God doesn't exist to fulfill our agendas; *we exist to get in touch with and fulfill His agenda.* What's on God's heart? The Bible doesn't tell us which car to buy or where to go on vacation, but it clearly spells out the things that are most important to God. Peter wrote, "The Lord is not slack concerning His promise, as some count slackness, but is longsuffering toward us, not willing that any should perish but that all should come to repentance" (2 Peter 3:9, *NKJV*).

WE KNOW GOD'S WILL IS FOR PEOPLE TO RESPOND TO HIS OFFER OF GRACE.

We know God's will is for people to respond to His offer of grace. He doesn't want anyone to go to hell. In Luke's account of the history of the Early Church, he tells us about many wonderful miracles that amazed people with the love and power of Christ. One day, Peter had a vision that led him to reach out to a Gentile soldier named Cornelius. As he explained the Gospel to Cornelius and his friends and family, Peter described the source of miraculous power: "God anointed Jesus of Nazareth with the Holy Spirit and power, and how He went around doing good and healing all who were under the power of the devil, because God was with Him" (Acts 10:38).

Whenever Jesus showed up and saw faith, He healed people. We know it's God's will to heal. Some spiritual things remain a mystery, but others are crystal clear. When we get in touch with God's mind, heart and agenda, amazing things happen. That's the kind of life I want to live. How about you?

There is something cleansing in knowing and meditating on His Word. The Lord does not condemn His children. He works all things for the good, and there isn't anything or anyone that can separate us from His love. His heavenly hygiene starts with salvation, but He continues to wash us through His Word and Spirit each day. That's why it is important to call upon the Lord at the start of each day. He is going to wash away the MV dirt in the mind and help you to identify old habits you need to eject and reject so you can inject new practices that strengthen your life with hope and faith.

FILLING UP THE EMPTY SPACES

Visualize for a moment that mind viruses are like drivers with cars pulling into a parking lot. These corrosive thoughts seek out the prime parking spots in the mind, and tenaciously wait for any opportunity to get one. Now in our physical world, I've seen people who drive onto our church property. They ride around looking for a parking space (preferably close to the sanctuary so they don't have to walk more than 100 feet). If they can't find a parking spot in our lot, they'll just leave. However, some people are persistent. After driving around and not finding a parking place anywhere, they will park a quarter mile away and walk to church. These are some very persistent people! Well, MVs are equally persistent.

I don't want MVs finding any empty spots in my mind's parking lot. I want all the empty spaces in my mind to be filled with God's wisdom, knowledge, and discernment. Memorizing and meditating on God's Word is like have new drivers and cars (new thoughts and practices) park in the mind—but the spaces have to be available. To be available means citing and towing away the MV practices that have parked in your mind's lot for ages. The easy MVs to eject are more distractions and bad habits. Some spend an incredible amount of time daydreaming about clothes, talking about sports, gossiping about people, or playing with new technology. Give these thoughts the spiritual citations from God's Word and they will leave. Yet, some spaces require a good tow and that involves letting the Holy Spirit work inside of you with prayer and His Word to do some incredible changes on focus and attitude. The major change is being able to forgive those who have wronged you. God forgives each of us for our sin, and we need to forgive our neighbors and family members.

All the mind virus families (fear, pride, despair) and their strains involving religious thinking have a dark undercurrent of bitterness. Sadly, people want payback—revenge—for what they perceive are wrongs done to them. The Bible is full of warnings about degenerating into a bitter and hard-hearted person. Here's one great passage to put to memory: "See, to it, brothers and sisters, that none of you has a sinful, unbelieving heart that turns away from the living God. But encourage one another daily, as long as it is called Today, so that none of you may be hardened by sin's deceitfulness" (Hebrews 3:12-13).

Marriage and Family Therapist J.E. Norris-Bernal brought up an excellent point from Pastor Lewis Smedes, a well-known theologian. He records Smedes saying, "Vengeance is having a videotape planted in your soul that cannot be turned off. It [revenge] plays the painful scene over and over again inside your mind and each time it plays you feel the clap of pain again. Forgiving turns off the videotape of pained memory. Forgiving sets you free."[21]

WASH UP

Listening to God's Word and the Holy Spirit about forgiving others will change you and drive out the worst of the MVs. Good maintenance of your mind requires you to focus on noble, praiseworthy and pure thoughts. Below is a short list of healthy routines that help:

1. **Rework your CD, DVD, and *cloud* library** material to reflect stories, themes and ideas that inspire you to love God and do what is right. Stories and music may deal with things, people and events that reflect struggles, hardship, ugliness and death. The question to always ask is: Does what you are listening and viewing encourage constructive (positive) thoughts or aggravate you toward destructive (negative) thoughts? *What's the final message reverberating in your brain?* The story of *Beauty and the Beast* is about someone ugly in appearance but beautiful inside. *The Narnia Chronicles* by C.S. Lewis have many characters based in mythology that emphasize virtues such as faithfulness, friendship and honesty. Bottom line: you have freedom in Christ to view and hear hard and gritty things in life, but *you are responsible for what you take into your mind and whether it helps you to become more like Christ.*

2. **Display and Play Scripture** in pictures, plaques, calendars, smartphone reminders, computer pop-ups, CDs, radio programs (any audio-visual print or electronic format). Place it in critical places at home, work, and in the car to refresh and remind you of God's love and His promises.

---

21. J.E. Norris-Bernal. *Forgiving Others and Trusting God.* (Xulon Press, 2011). p. 32.

3. **Write or Text Scripture** in your exhortation and comfort toward friends via cards, emails, and text messages. This practice is similar to the previous suggestion, but the emphasis is that you take time to write and text biblical passages that speak to you. The simply practice of writing, typing or texting God's Word is another means of remembering it in your mind. Searching to find the right passage to exhort someone else often leads you to study the Scriptures more and in greater detail.

4. **Establish a Daily Quiet Time** where you can meditate on Scripture. The quiet lets you focus on a passage and setting aside time makes the experience with God even more valuable to you. Meditative moments can be blended into times of gardening, driving, walking, workouts, etc. You can worship and meditate on God's Word at any time and in any environment—that is part of the great freedom you have in Christ.

5. **Put Bible Passages to Memory** and partner with someone who will do the same. That's right, forget your smartphone Bible verse reminder. Instead, put the Word directly into your memory. Memorizing Scripture can be like a spiritual *tuning fork* in your brain. You'll be tuned up to what is noble and right.

6. **Rework Your Personal Vocabulary** to reflect words that are accurate, constructive and visually powerful so that you can offer wisdom, comfort, admonishment and encouragement in the most powerful ways. Here are a number of words worth defining and integrating into everyday conversation: honorable, noble, trustworthy, gracious, merciful, kind, faithful, trustworthy and humble. Reworking the way you talk will affect other people. Season your language with what is good, inspiring and beautiful.

7. **Redeem the Good From all Circumstances.** Even when surrounded by negative people or difficult times, always pray to God and ask what can be learned. God is always working something good on your behalf.

8. **Go on Periodic Walks, Mini-Vacations and Field Trips** and surround yourself in all things that point to God's goodness, beauty, and His grace. Learn to take pleasure in watching living things; learn to appreciate the labor and craftsmanship to make things of beauty; learn to play games with your kids and friends and to share in the joy of the moment.

9. **Sing and Hum Hymns and Scripture-Based Songs** while sitting in a car, waiting room or walking. Singing and humming are relaxing and therapeutic for the mind and heart.

10. **Saturate Your Subconscious Mind** at bedtime with music or movies that are filled with wholesome values and laughter. Your subconscious is active even as you sleep and filling it with beautiful and inspiring things will affect you the following morning.

Changing the way we think (and consequently, how we feel and act) isn't rocket science. It's a simple matter of waste management: garbage in, garbage out. A lot of garbage is already in our minds, and it won't magically vanish. We have to grab it, throw it away, and put something else in its place. To do this, we need to forgive as Christ forgave us, feed our minds often and well with His Word, and listen to the Holy Spirit nudging us to do what is right. Use whatever tools in the physical world that will help to renew your mind. Each day we have to be conscientious as to what enters our mind to live a spiritually healthy life.

One of my favorite practices is to keep the radio in my car tuned to Christian music. It serves as the background noise in my life. By doing this, it helps me continually have praise, love, and glory in the back of my mind. I also have turned my car into a mobile seminary. I have messages of my favorite speakers on CDs or downloads, and I can listen to the best teachers whenever I want to. For me, this music and these messages are powerful medicine for my mind viruses. Of course, memorizing a Scripture a week is the best medicine of all. When basement voices came to Jesus, the voices were unsuccessful because He replied with this opening phrase over and over: "It is written." He fought mind viruses with the Word of God. We are wise to follow His example. If *it is written* in the Bible *it is written* by God— these are His love letters to show us the way of grace, mercy, love, wisdom and humility. There isn't any better way to live.

FURTHER DIAGNOSIS

1. How do you start your day with God?

2. Why do you think the Bible emphasizes going to God and His Word on a daily basis?

3. Have you ever tapped into your "Sixth Sense" with God? How is your life changed by being sensitive to the spiritual world around us?

4. Why is forgiveness important? What does the Bible say about forgiveness?

5. Do you think it's really possible to reprogram your unconscious mind? Why or why not? If you do, what are some practical things you can do to reprogram yours?

FILLING YOUR PRESCRIPTION

1. When you live exclusively by the physical world, you experience
    _____ _____.

2. I've placed my five senses in a _____ so they don't
    dominate my spiritual life.

3. The five senses are the way we navigate the _____
    world, but they are severely limited in helping us relate to the
    _____ world.

4. If you're confused by the term "living in the spirit", then think of it as
    living in the realm of the _____ sense.

5. A billion dollars can make you happy (at least for a while), but you
    would still be _____ by your five senses.

6. Tapping into the Spirit not only makes miracles possible – it makes
    them _____.

7. Spiritual connections are not visible to the eye, but they are even
    _____ _____ that a wireless connection.

8. One of the most important tasks for every believer is to _____
    our minds and hearts to be in touch with the spiritual world.

9. Changing the way we think isn't rocket science. It's a simple matter
    of _____ _____: garbage in, garbage
    out.

10. When basement voices came to Jesus, the voices were unsuccessful
    because He replied with this open phrase over and over: "_____
    _____ _____."

CHAPTER 9

YOUR CREATIVE POTENTIAL

"First comes thought; then organization of that thought into ideas and plans; then transformation of those plans into reality. The beginning, as you will observe, is in your imagination." — Napoleon Hill, American Motivational Writer, 1883-1970

A FEW YEARS AGO, it seems that the word *dream* was rediscovered. Hollywood producers put together a new production company called DreamWorks. Walt Disney World claimed to be the place *"Where dreams come true"* and had a Disney-on-Ice tour called *"Dare to Dream."* Agilent Technologies took up the slogan of *"Dreams made real"* while another company called Cadence asked, *"How big can you dream?"* The automaker Honda promoted the line *"The power of dreams."* I even used a slogan in one of our businesses: *"Teamwork makes the dream work."*

Corporations, Hollywood and theme parks don't have a monopoly on dreams. If anyone should be inspired to dream big dreams, it's those who are children of the Creator! If you know Jesus Christ, you have the Creator living inside you, and no one can match His infinite creativity. In the beginning, the Holy Spirit swept across the face of the deep and brought life to Earth. The magnificent beauty of His creation moves us to give glory to Him. Who would have thought of camels and spider monkeys? Who would have seen a world filled with naked mole rats and hippos, orchids and plankton? God did, and it's our delight to see the incredible wonders of His hand.

OUR CREATIVE CAPACITY

Human beings are created in the image of God. All of us—believers and unbelievers—have the capacity for amazing creativity. Christians have the additional capacity to tap into the heart of God and be even more imaginative! Everywhere we look, we see evidence of God's Creation and the works of men. Astronomers spend their careers trying to describe the wonders of the stars and galaxies. Modern telescopes enable us to observe the farthest reaches of the known galaxy. The distances are incomprehensible, and God has His hand on every atom. As we look around our homes and offices, we find modern marvels of creativity. The technological revolution of the past decades has made communication simple and quick. Our parents and grandparents couldn't have imagined the conveniences of smartphones and the Internet. Advances in medicine and every other field of science and industry have given us incredible marvels that make life easier. All of these are a reflection of the image of God—His amazing creativity—in people like you and me.

God hasn't stopped creating. He hasn't put a sign up that says He is closed to our imaginations. He desires to be a co-creator in each of our lives. In his letter to the Ephesians, Paul says that God formed each of us, and we have the privilege of joining Him as His partners. Paul wrote, "For we are His workmanship, created in Christ Jesus for good works, which God prepared beforehand so that we would walk in them" (Ephesians 2:10, *NASB*).

HOW CAN WE TELL IF AN IDEA IS FROM GOD? IT'S NOT ALWAYS EASY TO DISCERN.

How can we tell if an idea is from God? It's not always easy to discern the source of an idea. God gives us dreams, visions, and imagination, but our thoughts can be tainted by selfish ambition and other impure motivations. We can have many intrusions into our thoughts. When I'm thinking, praying, and meditating, I often get several thoughts that compete for my attention. To sort them out and analyze them, I write them down in a little black book. I carry it with me all the time. It houses my dreams and imaginations. If I get a *God thought*, I want to make sure I write it down. (God thoughts are usually easy to spot because I know I'm not that smart!). Someone said years ago: "A short pencil is better than long memory." That's true—writing it down in my book insures that my God thought won't be lost. Writing enables me to keep the ideas that are from the Lord and discard the ones that aren't. Some of my thoughts are simply today's version of a mind virus. I throw those in the trash, and I glue the good ones to my mind and heart.

USE YOUR FILTERS

Mind viruses, as we've seen, aren't harmless or neutral. They often seem good and right, but they destroy us and everything we hold dear. We need to use the filters of the Word, the Spirit, and mature Christian friends who give us feedback on our ideas. Many of the negative thoughts coming into our minds come from unwarranted fears, personal pride, and cynicism rooted in despair. If we let them, memories of the painful past turn into gripping fears of a terrible future. Little problems seem like catastrophes, and minor disagreements turn into World War III! We have a pain, and we worry about getting cancer. We have a spat with a spouse, and we think we're on the road to divorce. Our child has a bad day, and we imagine him being in prison for the rest of his life. Yes, there are real worries and concerns, but we need to sort out the ones that are real from the ones that are fear-prompted vanities. We need to refuse to let hurt, fear, anger, pride and discouragement dominate our thoughts. When I recognize them, I focus on the hope, joy, and dreams described in the Bible. I rivet my mind on God's love and a glorious future.

In *The God Nudge*, I explained that we are constantly listening to three voices: God's voice, the voice of evil, and our own voice. These voices shape our thoughts. When certain thoughts take root, our language and actions in the physical world are altered for good or evil. The trick with the voices is being mature and wise enough to discern who is talking. Let's take a look at these voices:

God's Voice - I know God's voice because I've spent time with Him in prayer and I've read His Word. I've learned to hear His voice and distinguish it from any other. His voice may be corrective, but it's always full of hope and love. Also, I can recognize God's voice when the answer is "yes" to these three questions:

• Does it line up with God's Word?

• Does it honor Jesus?

• Does it help others?

Evil's Voice - I can recognize the voice of evil because it spews condemnation, accusation, guilt, shame, and temptation. It either crushes me or prompts pride in my heart. As I'm speaking at a service, I may hear a voice in my mind that says, *Why don't you do this or say that so people will see how great you are?* That's from the pit of Hell! Evil's voice fails the tests of truth, love, justice, and mercy. Jesus said that everything the Evil One does is a lie; lying is the Devil's native tongue (see John 8:44). Gossip is a common voice of evil. I refuse to repeat innuendo and gossip. Spreading bad reports may be tempting, but it's playing into the enemy's hands.

Our Voice - Our internal dialogue is entirely familiar. It can be difficult to distinguish from God's voice and our voice. It's the one we've heard since we were born. Quite often, our voice is a reflection of our "old nature." It wants power, prestige, and pleasure. It is easily offended and wants revenge instead of seeking and giving forgiveness. Our voice wants credit for any success, and it wants to avoid blame for any mistake. The voice of our old nature longs to bask in the glow of others' admiration. It's devoid of humility.

Discerning what voices influence our behavior is important to stopping MVs, but it is also important for how we go about dreaming and imagining new things.

WHAT USED TO BE

Dreams die when the regrets and "what ifs" of the past contaminate them. If we live in the past, we can't dream of the future. I refuse to spend one more gallon of gas on my history. I've shifted to spending everything on my destiny. People may dwell on the past for many different reasons. For some, a past hurt is so bad they can't get it out of their minds. For others, a past failure is so devastating they can't get beyond it. Others look back at dumb decisions that have affected them for years, and some have never gotten over the loss of someone they love. It's perfectly fine to spend some time over how to heal pain, grieve over losses, forgive offenses, and tying up loose ends. However, it is completely crazy to spend all your time allowing your past dictate your future. That is not God's plan for us.

Each time one of those mind viruses appear, I counterattack with God's truth and love. I may be tempted to whine, "It's no use. I can't help it. I've always been that way." Yet, God helps me to respond to such foolishness. I remind myself, "Really? I have the power of the Creator living in me! I'm not helpless or hopeless! God talks to me about being bold and dreaming big. Ordinary people think with excuses, but I belong to God's family—extraordinary people—the children of the King!"

You may say, "My family has a long history of alcoholism and drug abuse. Now it looks like my kids are going to go down the same path." Yes, family patterns have an influence, but God's power to transform is far greater than that! Paul reminds us that God gives us a new start: "You have begun to live the new life, in which you are being made new and are becoming like the One who made you. This new life brings you the true knowledge of God (Colossians 3:10, *NCV*).

I can understand hopeless thinking if a person isn't a Christian. Yet, for those who have accepted Christ's sacrifice for their sins, the past---is past! When the hounds of hell come to pay a visit in your mind, don't engage them in conversation. Those voices have one purpose, and that's to devalue you. No matter how wicked you were and no matter how bad your circumstances are, God's grace wipes your slate clean. He sets you free and gives you a new purpose for living. Don't let sour self-talk bring you down any longer. You aren't the sum total of your past mistakes. YOU ARE A CHOSEN, ADOPTED, FORGIVEN, EMPOWERED CHILD OF GOD! Let that fact sink deep into your soul, and use this truth to combat every negative thought that bombards your mind. Don't sit and let those mind viruses loose in your thoughts. Fight back! Counterattack! And learn to live out God's dream for your life.

IMAGINE THE END RESULT

Instead of focusing our attention on the past, we need to invest our energies and hopes in a better future. When Wayne Dyer wrote *You Will See It When You Believe It*[22] and sent his manuscript to the publisher, Wayne was told he'd made a mistake in the title. The publisher thought Wayne had intended the title to read: "You Will Believe It When You See It." Wayne, however, knew what he wanted to convey and held to the original title.

Sometimes, we have to believe in something before we can see it. In Paul's letter to the Romans, he made the same point: "But hope that is seen is no hope at all. Who hopes for what they already have? But if we hope for what we do not yet have, we wait for it patiently" (Romans 8:24-25). If we want to have a vibrant spiritual life, we have to trust God even when we can't see any way He can come through for us. That's real faith.

There are times people suffer from sickness and disease for a long time. They've read the passages on healing. They've heard stories of God's miraculous intervention, but they're still sick. They're about to give up, but then they realize something has been missing—faith in God and His promises. They look at the familiar passages like the ones listed below,

---

22. Dyer. *You'll See It When You Believe It*

but now it is with a heart of faith. I was sick for a lengthy period of time. During those days, these Scriptures pulled me through to divine healing.

- "Jesus went throughout Galilee, teaching in their synagogues, proclaiming the good news of the kingdom, and *healing every disease* and sickness among the people" (Matthew 4:23).

- "but the crowds followed Him. He welcomed them and spoke to them about the kingdom of God, *and healed those who needed healing*" (Luke 9:11).

- "By faith in the name of Jesus, this man who you see and know was made strong. It is Jesus' name and the faith that comes through Him that *has given this complete healing to him*, as you can all see" (Acts 3:16).

- "God anointed Jesus of Nazareth with the Holy Spirit and power, and how He went around doing good and *healing all* who were under the power of the devil, because God was with Him" (Acts 10:38).

- " 'Have faith in God,' Jesus answered. 'Truly, I tell you, if anyone says to this mountain, 'Go, throw yourself into the sea,'" and does not doubt in his heart but believe that what He says will happen, it will be done for them. Therefore, I tell you, whatever you ask for in prayer, *believe that you have received it*, and it will be yours' " (Mark 11:22-24).

- "Surely He has borne our griefs and carried our sorrows; yet we esteem Him stricken, smitten by God, and afflicted. But He was wounded for our transgressions, He was bruised for our iniquities; the chastisement for our peace was upon Him, and *by His stripes we are healed*" (Isaiah 53:4-5, *NKJV*).

- "Then He said to him [the leper], 'Rise and go; *your faith has made you well*' " (Luke 17:19).

- "The man went away and told the Jewish leaders that *it was Jesus who had made him well*" (John 5:15).

When our emotions match up with our mind's knowledge and we act upon those promises, amazing things happen. Our hope rises and our capacity to dream again takes flight because we know God hears our prayers and responds to our faith.

Throughout the Bible, the writers go to great lengths to expand our concept of the greatness and grace of God. They use language that suggests they had a hard time putting God's majesty into words. For example, at the end of one of his prayers for the Christians in Ephesus, Paul concluded, "God can do anything, you know—far more than you could ever imagine or guess or request in your wildest dreams!" (Ephesians 3:20, *The Message*).

Imagination is potent when sparked by God and directed to Him in prayer. It is a MV vaccine of incredible power. Let me share some rules about the importance of having a sharp and God-focused imagination.

RULE #1: IMAGINATION IS MORE IMPORTANT THAN KNOWLEDGE.

While watching the blockbuster movie, *Spiderman*, I saw an inscription on a poster in Peter Parkers' bedroom wall. It was a quote by Albert Einstein: "Imagination is more important than knowledge." I'd heard a similar statement attributed to Einstein: "Knowledge will get you from point A to B, but imagination is limitless." I think he was on to something!

One of the greatest gifts you were ever given is the gift of imagination. Just look around you. All the advances in science, technology, art, and medicine were once in someone else's imagination—in the mind of inventors, scientists, and architects, or in the mind of God. William Blake commented, "What is now proved was once imagined." You are closest to God's mind and heart when you are imagining and partnering with God to create something new.

> **ONE OF THE GREATEST GIFTS YOU WERE EVER GIVEN IS THE GIFT OF IMAGINATION.**

Mind viruses kill imagination. Actually, that's only partially true. They can compel our imagination to selfish endeavors. They twist our motives and enflame our self-absorbed passions. But they destroy our thoughts of doing wonderful things out of glad obedience for the glory of God. The solution: Take charge of your imagination. Your imagination is limitless, but the stress and strain of life can erode our hopes and dampen our enthusiasm to imagine new and better things. Some people become more creative with age, but most of us suffer from creative atrophy as we get older. When we were children, we could think of all kinds of wild ideas and projects. As we grew older, however, we became more skeptical (even cynical), we started following existing patterns of thought instead of challenging them, and our imagination began to go dark.

A perceptive person once said, "If you want your children to be intelligent, read them fairy tales. If you want them to become more intelligent, read them more fairy tales." Kids need to have permission to dream and imagine limitless things. In countless ways, they'll learn that some ideas don't work. But don't rush to stop their creative juices from flowing! Give them room to dream, imagine, and create—even if they mess up the living room with their creations.

RULE #2: PLACE A DO NOT DISTURB SIGN AT THE DOOR OF IMAGINATION.

It's easy to drift into complacency and let habits dictate our thoughts. To combat this drift, I've placed a "Do Not Disturb" sign over the door of my imaginations. I won't let anybody keep me from dreaming big dreams. Sure, not all of them will work out, but who cares? It's far better to dream big and fall a little short than to remain in a creative straightjacket. Mind viruses of doubt and discouragement can come from within our own thoughts, but too often, those who think they know best how to run our lives try to convince us that our dreams simply can't come true. Don't listen to these voices! Guard your imagination as a sacred gift from God. Feed it, nurture it, and let it thrive. Some of your dreams will become your most cherished legacy. President Theodore Roosevelt famously said, "Far better it is to dare mighty things, to win glorious triumphs even though checkered by failure, than to rank with those timid spirits who neither enjoy nor suffer much because they live in the gray twilight that knows neither victory nor defeat."[23]

Your imagination is fertile soil you are preparing so you can plant new, bold dreams. You've spent a considerable amount of time preparing your garden. Weeds have been yanked out, fertilizer has been spread, and the ground is ready for seeds. At this point, you wouldn't allow someone walking down the street to plant weeds in your garden, would you? Of course not. That would be ludicrous. From this day forward, live by this motto: "I

23. Roosevelt, Theodore. "Dare Mighty Things." The Man in the Arena: Citizenship in a Republic. Apple Seeds. Updated October 29, 2014. Accessed November 6, 2014. http://www.appleseeds.org/DareRoos.htm

will never, never, never allow anyone to pollute my imagination. No one has the right to come in and plant his seeds in the soil that I have so meticulously prepared. I've prepared the soil, and I'll choose what to plant there. And I choose big dreams for God's purposes!" Many of us let others sow doubt into our gardens because we're insecure. We don't have enough confidence to take control of our dreams. As we grow stronger in God's love and strength, He'll give us more confidence to dream big dreams.

The death of the power to dream can come early in life. Young people often feel pulled apart by conflicting dreams and agendas. If they're not careful, they can listen to the wrong voices and miss the dream God has put on their hearts. When I was in my twenties, I was in Bible school. At one point, I visited my mom and brother who lived in East Texas. Their church asked me to preach on Sunday morning. After the service, a man invited me to join him for coffee. After we sat down, he told me, "I want to show you a church I've built." I was a young minister and very interested in new, creative ways of planting and building churches. After we left the coffee shop, he drove us to a new church building. He turned to me and announced, "Son, I'm convinced God wants you to be the pastor of this church."

I have to confess, it was very tempting. I thought about it for a moment, and then I responded, "Thank you for your offer. I really appreciate it, but it's not what God has put on my heart. I'm afraid I'll have to say no." He was very surprised. I explained that I needed to finished my Bachelor's Degree and complete my education. He wasn't convinced. You see, he had an agenda for my life, but his agenda was going to be at the expense of my destiny. I chose God's agenda and my dreams over his designs. It was a good move.

RULE #3: DON'T ALLOW CURRENT CONDITIONS TO RESTRICT YOUR IMAGINATION.

Our DNA shapes our lives in significant ways, but so does our environment. A person born in our country in this era has infinitely more resources and opportunities than someone born in Tibet in the twelfth century. And the person born today has many more distractions, too. Our culture, family relationships, close friendships, economic conditions, and other factors can all shape our imaginations—for better or for worse. In important ways, I am who I am today because of the people who have influenced me. I am a product of the influences of everything and everybody I've experienced throughout my lifetime.

Environment is powerful, but it isn't completely dominating. We can change the trajectory of our lives. The Bible uses different terms for this change. We repent by turning from sin to the love and forgiveness of God, and we become disciples by wanting God's will with all our hearts. If our lives are stuck in the mud, we can sit around and complain about "bad parents" and "bad breaks," but staying there is our own choice. Others may have had a significant and negative impact, but no one is keeping us stuck. If I don't like where I am today, then I'm to blame. People have all kinds of excuses and rationalizations for staying stuck. I don't buy them. The love of Jesus frees us, and the power of the Spirit enables us to get up and get going in a new direction. Our future depends on the choices we make today! If you want greater things in life, you have to challenge the lies you believe. Unchallenged belief systems have destroyed and defeated countless people.

Instead of being bold and optimistic, it's a lot easier to blame others for our problems or live in hopeless despair. When I meet people who are struggling with life, some of them tell me, "I'm afraid this is just the way things are. I can't change anything." With that attitude, they're right! But with a fresh injection of hope and courage, anything is possible. Actually,

I believe that change should be normal—especially for Christians. Paul talked about the "fruit of the Spirit." Fruit grows gradually, seasonally and inevitably. If a fruit tree isn't producing fruit, it's dead or dying. I don't want to live like that. I believe God wants us to have a sense of "holy discontent" so we're always reaching, always striving, always pursuing greater dreams.

CREATIVITY BEGINS WITH YOUR SPIRIT.

Creativity begins with your spirit. Your spirit, like your imagination, is dealing with invisible matter. Creativity, then, goes even beyond the five senses. Our five senses are wonderful gifts from God, but we're primarily spiritual creatures. If we rely solely on our senses, they can become a barrier to imagination. We need to ask God to give us ideas and impressions that transcend the physical world. The source of true life, hope, love, and creativity is the Spirit of God. Jesus explained, "It is the Spirit who gives life." (John 6:63, *NKJV*).

Karen and I have the privilege of leading a great church in Central California. We have four services each weekend, and we're running out of room for new people. Years ago our leadership realized we needed a new worship center. We believe God wants us to be a church of 10,000 people, so we designed plans for a new 3,000-seat auditorium and figured we could run three services in the larger facility.

There's only one problem. We needed $4 million in the bank before we begin. When I began writing this manuscript, we did not have the money. Now, three years later we have the money to begin. We did not let financial circumstances and hurdles become the demise of our dream. From the outset, we believed God was going to provide. After all, it's His vision, His agenda, His money, and His heart for every person in our community. In an effort to strengthen the dream (even as we broke ground in 2014), I had already envisioned preaching my first sermon in the new worship center. In my mind, I stand where the pulpit will be. I preach my heart out, give the altar call, and people are born again! The future fulfillment of the dream is so real to me that I can almost touch it. Of course, the enormity of the project makes my five senses scream, "No!" Yet, my Spirit-inspired imagination built on God's Word shouts, "Yes!"

TICKER TAPE

I can allow my life to be limited by my five senses or my imagination can become a co-creator with God. I compare my thoughts each day to the New York Stock Exchange ticker tape. In the old days, there was actual tape coming out of a device. Today, it's electronic. You can see it on the cable financial stations at the bottom of the screen. If you watch long enough, you'll see how individual stocks are performing at that moment. Private investors don't care much about 99 percent of the companies that appear on the screen, but every now and then the company they've invested in shows up. Now you've got their attention! Why? Because that is where they're personally invested.

Try to picture your thoughts like a ticker tape. Have you noticed that you have about five negative thoughts to each positive one? Smart investors dump losers and pick winning stocks. It's the same for you and me in our mental investments. We need to dump the losers and invest in winners. For instance, after I've been awake for an hour, I can usually identify six different thoughts that have been rummaging in my head: sadness, fear, discouragement, resentment, gratitude, and shame. Which of these pays healthy dividends? It's pretty easy to pick the winner, isn't it? Why in the world would I stay invested in the other five? It's foolish, and it would ruin the rest of my day. No, I'm going to choose "gratitude" today. I'm making a conscious decision that I'm going to be thankful and hang around with people who are joyful, thankful, positive people.

This process of change isn't a mystery. It's common sense. The pathway for the day begins with the thoughts you choose. You should focus your attention on thoughts that reflect the greatness and grace of God. Consider His values in relationships and show integrity in all you do. Here's how you do it:

- First, identify the positive thought.

- Second, contemplate what it will look like to live according to it.

- Third, make the choice to focus your mind and heart on the thought and how you will live it out in every action, attitude, and relationship.

We can't keep negative thoughts from popping into our heads, but we have the responsibility and power to choose which ones to keep and which to eliminate. For instance, if a dark thought of condemnation, guilt, and shame invades your mind, identify it, focus on the truth from God's Word about forgiveness, and then live it out. There are many passages you could use, but I like these two: "Therefore, there is now no condemnation for those who are in Christ Jesus..." (Romans 8:1), and "Therefore, if anyone is in Christ, he is a new creature; the old things passed away; behold, new things have come!" (2 Corinthians 5:17, *NASB*). Guilt and condemnation feel very normal to many of us, but they poison our souls. Don't let them linger! Notice them on the ticker tape and replace them with the life-changing truth of the Gospel of Jesus Christ. Invest in the dreams rooted in your identity in God. Fuel your dreams with the promises God gives and then be bold enough to take steps of faith.

> **WE CAN'T KEEP NEGATIVE THOUGHTS FROM POPPING INTO OUR HEAD, BUT WE HAVE THE POWER TO CHOOSE WHICH ONES TO KEEP AND WHICH TO ELIMINATE.**

NEW CHOICES, NEW HABITS

Negative patterns of thinking are deeply entrenched in our lives. They don't vanish with a single prayer or an isolated choice. We have to create new, healthy habits of the mind by making hundreds—actually, thousands—of choices. Then the new choices gradually become new, healthy habits. We can't just add new behaviors to old ones and hope to get a different result. Two things can't occupy the same parking space in our minds! As we make new choices, we have to stop giving time, attention, and energy to the old, destructive ones. For instance, if you want to avoid tension in a marriage, you have to stop griping about the little things that annoy you. You have to replace those comments with affirmation and gratitude toward your spouse. (And then pick your spouse up after he or she faints!)

In Paul's letter to the Ephesians, he uses a metaphor of changing clothes. He says to "put off" sinful attitudes and behaviors, and "put on" ones that reflect the love and power of Christ. He told the Christians to stop lying and speak the truth, to stop letting anger poison relationships but deal with it quickly, to stop stealing but earn a living and generously share with others, to stop wielding words as weapons but use them to give love and life, and finally, to get rid of bitterness, and instead, to forgive in the same way Jesus has forgiven us (see Ephesians 4:20-32). Paul gave five clear examples, but of course, there are many more times and situations when we need to make choices to "put off" the old and "put on" the new. His point is that each of us has definite choices all day every day. What choices will we make? To avoid making a choice is a choice, too.

If you want to stop an old habit, you have to start a new habit. We have a slogan at our church: "Give us a year of your life, and you will never be the same." I tell people, "If you'll make two new, good choices each week, your life will be radically changed in ninety days." The options are almost endless. They can get involved in Weekend Life and Weekday Life at our church, regularly attend services on the weekend, or join a Bible study during the week. Some people offer excuses. They sometimes tell me, "Pastor, I have too many bad habits. It's hard to get up on Sundays. And besides, I don't want to go to a Bible study because I don't want people to know my secrets." These people don't understand that church is specifically *for* people with bad habits. Perfect people need not apply!

It takes more than will power to break deeply entrenched bad habits. Plenty of people have tried really hard and failed. They have to be gradually replaced with new, healthy habits. When we create a new habit, the old habit will eventually fade away. That's a way to stop a mind virus—through starvation. If you starve the bad habit and start feeding a new, good habit, you make real progress. God has given you an arsenal of tools to destroy the old habits and to nurture the good ones through Scripture, prayer, fellowship, music, worship and evangelism—any of these dynamic parts of life coupled with imagination and dreams to honor God and His Kingdom has an enormous effect in healing a person.

RETRAIN THE MIND

Earlier in the book I mentioned how our mind works much like a computer. Today, computers in the average car are more powerful and sophisticated than the one used to take the Apollo 11 landing craft to the moon! But computers can give faulty readings. The one in Karen's car constantly told her she had a flat tire. When it first flashed, we walked around the car to inspect each tire. They all looked fine. When the signal didn't go out, we checked the air pressure in each one. They were all fine. I thought that maybe if I kicked the tires real hard, it would jar the computer and the light would stop flashing. That didn't work either. All day, every day, for many weeks, the same message appeared on her dash: YOUR TIRE PRESSURE IS LOW. Then it hit me: Karen's car had a mind virus. We finally took the car to the dealer. The repair shop took it for a day. The technician retrained the computer, and it's worked fine since then.

The question for us is "How do you retrain the computer between your ears?" Your mind automatically thinks in habitual patterns. Your brain records every decision you make, and your mind repeats what it records. Have you ever noticed how many days you choose to wear the same clothes in a week or month? Why the repetition? Your brain is programmed to make the same choices based on certain criteria.

In doing research for this book, I have read more than once that we don't use our brain to its fullest capacity. Now there are a lot of jokes, I could insert right here, but let's just suffice it to say that we use approximately 5 percent of the total workings of our brain while leaving 95 percent untapped. So 5 percent is conscious and 95 percent is subconscious! God has given us an incredible gift, our brain, and some of us don't even use the 5 percent properly! As I noted earlier in the book, some of our mental programming can be affected through your subconscious mind which is very open to suggestions. For this reason, listening to some inspiring recording (music, preaching, teaching, testimony or story) or viewing something that is beautiful and points to God's provision and creativity (a painting, a movie, a photo of a trip or someone you love, looking at a child in its cradle, etc.) right before you go to bed will influence you when you wake up. Contemplating good thoughts before you fall asleep will affect your behavior when you rise the next day.

These little practices before bedtime may seem trivial at first, but you can tap into your subconscious mind and fix it. At first, it may seem like a man trying to fix a toaster in your next-door neighbor's house while standing in your living room. It seems almost impossible; but I think with God all things are possible! We all know bad habits don't die easily so you have to attack it at a subconscious level, and when you awake in the morning take small steps to change your direction to a lifestyle that is whole.

> IT SEEMS ALMOST IMPOSSIBLE; BUT I THINK WITH GOD ALL THINGS ARE POSSIBLE!

I spoke recently to a fellow who is struggling with a self-defeating habit, and walks around in defeat. His head bowed low and eyes fixed on looking at his feet (de-feat—do you get it?) Anyway, he thinks it's impossible to win the battle over his long-time friend; *a self-destructive behavior.* I suggested that he take seven days and begin to change something small that would head him in the direction of right behavior. If you're thinking that seven days is too long to begin to make a change then break it down into smaller hills to climb. Why not see if you can go 72 hours without doing that bad habit. Why not try seven hours. It all begins with baby steps. I think any habit can be broken if we learn to retrain the brain. The American writer Mark Twain said it best: "Habit is habit, and not to be flung out of the window by any man, but coaxed downstairs a step at a time."[24]

Old habits are broken by using your subconscious and conscious mind, using approaches that inspire, invigorate and renew you to begin a process of dreaming. The by-product of constructive dreams and beautiful imaginations is hope. You begin to think about a new job, a new way to tackle a problem, a new day to bring people together or a new relationship that brings you joy. God's faithfulness to each us is new each

24. Twain, Mark. "Habit." Mark Twain Quotations, Newspaper Collections, & Related Sources: Habit. Updated April 9, 1997. Accessed November 5, 2014. http://www.twainquotes.com/Habit.html

morning—we're always on a fresh slate with God, and He asks us to renew our minds each day to have a fresh attitude towards Him and others.

Mind viruses give way to mind virtues. The whole process up to this chapter in Mind Viruses is boiled down for you on the list below:

- *Always Identify The Motivators*—What are the voices of good or evil in and around you suggesting you do?

- *Check Your Attitude*—a real thermostat to what you are thinking is how your attitude is either destroying or uplifting those around you. Is it garbage in and your mouths spews the garbage out, or is it wholesome in and your tongue exhorts others to love and good deeds in Christ. Which is it?

- *Learn to Focus*—Concentrate on learning what kind of man or woman God wants you to be. Don't get distracted, but be persistent in growing in Christ. If you hit a setback, get right up and keeping walking with God.

- *Starve Bad Habits, Plant New Ones*—Use God's tools that challenge and uproot your negative and destructive thoughts. Engage the subconscious and conscious mind with beautiful and inspiring material.

- *Unleash God-Rich Imagination*—Flood your mind with good dreams and imaginative approaches to honor the Lord as you dwell on Scripture, sing praise, share Christ, and listen to wisdom. Your output of hope will skyrocket and will act as a supernatural vaccine on your mindscape.

Remember you are a new creation that can do all things through Christ because He strengthens you. Dream! Dream big! Imagine the wonderful and pursue it with the Lord whose name is Wonderful.

FURTHER DIAGNOSIS

1. Do you have a hope or a dream that you share with the Lord in prayer? What is it?

2. Have you ever offered a friend imaginative solutions in how to grow in God? If so, what ideas did you generate?

3. Has God given you a dream? If so, what is hindering or helping you in accomplishing that dream?

4. How have you attacked an old, destructive habit and replaced it with a new one in Christ?

5. How did God introduce hope in your own life?

FILLING YOUR PRESCRIPTION

1. If anyone should be inspired to dream big dreams, it's those who are _____ of the Creator!

2. We are constantly listening to three voices: _____ voice, the voice of evil, and our own voice.

3. I can recognize God's voice when the answer is "yes" to these three questions:

• Does it _____ _____ with God's Word?

• Does it _____ Jesus?

• Does it _____ others?

4. Our voice wants power, prestige, and _____.

5. I refuse to spend one more gallon of gas on my _____.

6. _____ will get you from point A to point B, but imagination is limitless.

7. I've placed a "____ _____ _____" sign over the door of my imagination.

8. Live by this motto: "I will never, never, never allow anyone to _____ my imagination.

9. He had an agenda for my life, but his agenda was going to be at the _____ of my destiny.

10. We can sit around and complain about "bad parents" and "bad breaks", but staying there is our own _____.

11. If you want to stop an old habit, you have to start a _____ habit.

the plan of God. There's a timing and rhythm to creating something great. You have to get in sync with your teammates and the only way you're going to do that is by spending the time and effort required in intentional training. There's absolutely no substitute for training. In training we get in step with the timing, and the process, and the thinking of our various team members. We are all working, we are all training, together.

Not only is it important to work together, but we all must find our individual destinies. You and I are made in the image of God. We're on loan to the people of the earth. Mark Twain observed, "The two most important days of your life are the day you were born and the day you figured out why." If you can discover why you were placed on the planet, you'll tap into an unlimited supply of spiritual power outside your five senses.

People may look very different, but if you peel back the layers of race, age, gender, and culture, we have a lot in common. We long to love and be loved, and we want to live for something higher and greater than ourselves. We may have been born at different times and in different places, but our hearts' desires are the same. We have the privilege and responsibility to chart our own paths. When it is all said and done, all of us have a story to tell based on individual experiences and environment.

However, we're all not going down the same road toward the same destination. Some have committed themselves to acquiring power, some want positions of prestige, and some crave pleasure at all costs. We used to be in one of those categories, but Jesus changed our hearts and destinies. He also changed our traveling companions. To achieve our dreams—our God-inspired dreams—we need each other. It's not an option. Wouldn't it be fantastic if we found others with the same passions, desires and values? Many of us have found those people. We understand the exponential power of joining forces and journeying together. That's what the Church is all about. It's not a building or a set of programs. It's about people helping other people walk with God and fulfill their dreams. I love the Psalms and one of my favorite passages praises the power of positive relationships.

How good and pleasant it is when God's people live together in unity! It is like precious oil poured on the head, running down on the beard, running down on Aaron's beard, down on the collar of his robe. It is as the dew of Hermon were falling on Mount Zion. For there the LORD bestows His blessing, even life forevermore (Psalm 133:1-3).

God wants us to find other believers who support us and who are willing for us to support them. We don't have to be clones. It's more exciting if we're different enough to bring new ideas, but similar enough to understand each other—that's *synchro-destiny*. We love, affirm, encourage, and help each other toward our God-honoring destinies. That's God's plan for a group of believers. Of course, when "iron sharpens iron," there are sometimes sparks, but that's where we learn even more to love, trust and communicate.

Many young people need the help and support of those who are a little farther down the road. In our culture of easy divorce, many young adults are scared to get married. They don't want to become a statistic like their parents, their friends' parents or their friends whose marriages didn't work out. My friend, Dr. Kermit Bridges, serves as president of Southwestern Assemblies of God College in Waxahachie, Texas. He observes that young people between the ages of 16 and 26 are in the decade of decision. He explains that in our youth we make three major decisions that influence the direction and course of our lives:

- Will you make Jesus Christ your Lord?

- What career will you choose (and which college will help you realize that dream)?

- Whom will you marry if you choose to get married?

Young people don't need older Christians to preach at them about relationships and career choices. As they wade into the deep waters of permanent relationships, what they seek is love, understanding, and patience. They need a community of trusted people to help them make wise decisions; they need support to do the right things in life.

It's not just young people who need strong affirming relationships. To achieve our dreams, we have to find people to walk with us. In his letter to the Ephesians, Paul encouraged leaders to get involved in equipping, building and strengthening others. There are many different leaders and leadership styles in the Church. Some of the most effective leaders are those who don't have official titles. As we get involved in people's lives, our role is to encourage them…

…until we all reach unity in the faith and in the knowledge of the Son of God and become mature, attaining to the whole measure of the fullness of Christ. Then we will no longer be infants, tossed back and forth by the waves, and blown here and there by every wind of teaching and by the cunning and craftiness of people in their deceitful scheming. Instead, speaking the truth in love, we will grow to become in every respect the mature body of Him who is the head, that is, Christ. From Him the whole body, joined and held together by every supporting ligament, grows and builds itself up in love, as each part does its work (Ephesians 4:13-16).

I was watching Wayne Dyer on PBS Television and he used this illustration:

Imagine for a moment that you find yourself with a flashlight in your hand. The room is totally dark. You turn your light on and see a beautiful painting hanging on the wall. You marvel at such a wonderful work of art. Then someone turns the room light on. You're no longer constrained to view just one painting lit by a flashlight, but see around you an art museum with hundreds of beautiful paintings.

That is the same illumination you get in the promise of meaningful, intimate, God-focused relationships—we see much more than ever before. As we see ourselves and others through the loving eyes of our friends, we are given the ability to see the whole picture of our destiny. The lights go on and the flashlight becomes irrelevant.

This isn't a pipedream. This is the picture the Bible paints of the kind of connections we can and should have in the Body of Christ. Can you imagine the impact of this kind of relationship on you, your family, your church and city? People would feel secure enough to dream again. They'd take bold steps without being terrified of failing because they'd know the people who love them will pick them up if they fall. These people would pray and encourage each other, and they'd celebrate like crazy over each step forward in each person's life. Don't you want to be part of something like that?

> **MIND VIRUSES CANNOT THRIVE IN A SOUL BLESSED WITH A STEADY STREAM OF HEAVENLY THOUGHTS THAT CLEAN AND NOURISH.**

The spillover into society is profound. Christians in unity and loving each other to fulfill their destinies in God creates rivers of living water that touch the lives of those who still may not know Him. It is purified water. It is the best water because it comes from the true Rock of Ages—Jesus. Mind viruses cannot thrive in a soul blessed with a daily stream of heavenly thoughts that clean and nourish.

MORE THAN ONE STANDS TO GAIN OR LOSE

Negative thoughts—destructive mind viruses—not only rob us of achieving all we are created for, the MVs also immobilize our role in affecting our family, schools, churches, workplaces and nation. What we all stand to gain or lose in the war against mind viruses involves more than our own life. Jesus, in one of His most famous stories, talks about the importance of being faithful and true in growing and nurturing what has been given to your care. Jesus uses the story of a boss who gave his employees instruction on investing his money to illustrate the importance of being a good steward:

> Again, it will be like a man going on a journey, who called his servants and entrusted his wealth to them. To one he gave five bags of gold, to another two bags, and to another one bag, each according to his ability. Then he went on his journey. The man who had received five bags of gold went at once and put his money to work and gained five bags more. So also, the one with two bags of gold gained two more. But the man who had received one bag went off, dug a hole in the ground and hid his master's money.

> After a long time the master of those servants returned and settled accounts with them. The man who had received five bags of gold brought the other five. "Master," he said, "you entrusted me with five bags of gold. See, I have gained five more."

> His master replied, "Well done, good and faithful servant! You have been faithful with a few things; I will put you in charge of many things. Come and share your master's happiness!"

> The man with two bags of gold also came. "Master," he said, "you entrusted me with two bags of gold; see, I have gained two more."

> His master replied, "Well done, good and faithful servant! You have been faithful with a few things; I will put you in charge of many things. Come and share your master's happiness!"

> Then the man who had received one bag of gold came. "Master," he said, "I knew that you are a hard man, harvesting where you have not sown and gathering where you have not scattered seed. So I was afraid and went out and hid your gold in the ground. See, here is what belongs to you."

His master replied, "You wicked, lazy servant! So you knew that I harvest where I have not sown and gather where I have not scattered seed? Well then, you should have put my money on deposit with the bankers, so that when I returned I would have received it back with interest. So take the bag of gold from him and give it to the one who has ten bags. For whoever has will be given more, and they will have an abundance. Whoever does not have, even what they have will be taken from them. And throw that worthless servant outside, into the darkness, where there will be weeping and gnashing of teeth" (Matthew 25:14-30).

Each of these employees was given a sum of money to invest while the boss was out of town. When the boss returned, he found that two of his servants made good investments. The third servant, however, didn't fare as well. He buried his investment in the ground without investing it. When the boss asked him about his choice, he rationalized, "I was afraid and went and hid your talent in the ground." The internal dialogue in his mind was shaped by fear, not faith.

It is important to understand that what we have been given in our lives was not only to bless us, but is designed to affect other people. Defeating mind viruses is not only a victory for yourself, but it is a victory that affects your family, friends, acquaintances and even enemies at home, in the workplace, on the field, at church and in the nation. Everyone gains when you stop your mind viruses; everyone is blessed when you replenish your mind with those things that God finds pleasure in.

A RIGHT WORD MAKES A WORLD OF DIFFERENCE

When MVs are being uprooted and your mind is filled with good, creative and inspiring thoughts, the most obvious barometer that measures that change is found in your speech. Jesus told His followers that "A good man out of the good treasure of his heart brings forth what is good; and the evil man out of the evil treasure brings forth what is evil; for his mouth speaks that which fill his heart" (Luke 6:45, *NASB*).

The words we speak reveal the condition of our mind and heart. Those of us who are discouraged and depressed tell tales of our sorrow and hardship. Our tongue describes our deep-hearted aches and exposes our fears to take any further risks in life. Those of us who have been emotionally and physically hurt employ words calculated to keep people at a distance.

Our tongue uses words to shield us from having to be vulnerable toward another human being. Those of us who are bitter wait for someone to ignite our anger. When the fuse is lit, we explode into a flurry of words that condemn, mock and even, at times, hate. Of course, there are many variations of these conditions and expressions of the mind and heart, but the principle is clear: Our words reflect the health of our inner man. Our words affect the world around us.

As God daily transforms our minds on the inside then the words we use will also change. These positive words coupled with acts of love and humility can change the landscape of our family interactions. It can alter how coworkers perceive our actions; it can shape creative outcomes and political directions. It isn't by accident that Paul reminds us: "Let your conversation be always full of grace, seasoned with salt, so that you may know how to answer everyone" (Colossians 4:6).

Knowing who you are in God and His destiny for you transforms your everyday speech. Why is that important? Because the Gospel of Christ is carried by you, His chosen ambassador, to the friends on the bowling team, folks at the grief ministry, buddies at school, people at the coffee shop, the doctor at the clinic, and on and on. The whole world turns right-side-up when your everyday conversation is filled with words that are uplifting. As MVs are banished, we find our identity in God becomes stronger. Here's what Paul said to the Christians in Ephesus:

> You were taught, with regard to your former way of life, to put off your old self, which is being corrupted by its deceitful desires; to be made new in the attitude of your minds; and to put on the new self, created to be like God in true righteousness and holiness. Therefore each of you must put off falsehood and speak truthfully to your neighbor, for we are all members of one body (Ephesians 4:22-25).

For genuine and lasting change to occur, you have to realize that your thinking (which is reflected in your words) is too much like "your former way of life"—unforgiving, critical, judgmental, and harsh. You need to partner with the Spirit of God to transform your mind—the way you think about God's love, forgiveness, purpose, and peace—so your words communicate grace and truth to those around you. The Christian life is often compared to a race. Until you make a conscious effort to select a new lane to run in, you're headed to the wrong destination. Your tongue—what you say and how you say it—is either venting poisonous speech from your old self or providing God's living water.

GENERATIONAL PAINS AND JOYS

As a pastor, I see this pattern all too often with MVs—the power of negative thoughts, translated into negative words, attitudes and habits can affect spouses, children, and grandchildren and carry potency across generations. For instance, take a wife who is constantly nagging her husband about everything. It seems he can't do anything right. She doesn't like the way he chews his food, the television shows he prefers, the way he walks, talks, handles money or relates to the children. Sure, he has faults, but he's trying to be a good husband and father. The problem isn't him, it's her. She has graduated as the valedictorian from Fault Finder University with a major in criticism! She aced those courses! Her husband will grapple with those negative memories for a long time if she keeps pounding into her husband's head that "he's a failure."

Men aren't the only victims. Consider a husband who constantly belittles his wife about the way she keeps house, the clothes she wears, how she cooks, the way she spends money, and her choice of friends. He demands that she change. Of course, she has flaws, but his demeanor doesn't invite dialogue and the pursuit of common ground. His criticism makes her angry, hurt, and even more defiant than ever. In time, she's becomes determined to make his life miserable out of spite and revenge. He has poisoned his wife's attitude with such venom that she'll be detoxing with friends for years about the pain, and often will produce her own root of bitterness that sours children, family and close friends. In these scenarios, nobody wins.

You may be thinking, "If these people would dedicate their lives to Jesus, then all that would change." I'm here to tell you that it doesn't. When Jesus comes into a person's life, the old nature doesn't suddenly evaporate. It's still there. Spiritual growth is the daily application of the power and love of the Gospel to every area of life. One of the most challenging areas of life—for all of us—is the reality of entrenched mind viruses that have shaped our thoughts, feelings, and responses throughout our lives. A lot of people have dedicated their lives to Christ, but their old nature is dominating their thoughts, attitudes and speech to people. MVs affect more than our mind—it corrupts relationship, families, communities and even a nation. Imagine how that world around us may be affected by one man or woman filled with Christ-rich thoughts.

In the Bible, Abraham's faith in God not only transformed his life, but it created a legacy with his descendants. His son Isaac and grandson Jacob found a firm foundation in Abraham's example. Consider King David, too. When the MVs got the best of him, David made big mistakes. When his mind was focused on God and His will, David made great decisions. His failures with Bathsheba (letting his MVs run wild) led to family problems including with his first child with Bathsheba. Later in life, David's oldest son Amnon would rape his half-sister. His other son Absalom would then kill Amnon and lead an insurrection against David.

DAVID'S EXAMPLE

David, however, did one thing right. Over and over, he went back to God for forgiveness and strength (take a peek at Psalm 51). He came to understand the importance of daily connecting with God regardless of the problems or successes around him. Even when David was an old man, he remained a spitfire—a guy full of energy—wanting to honor God. Of course, David made many mistakes in his life. Sometimes the mind viruses took the best of him, but David always humbly went back to the Lord for direction. Loving God was where his heart thrived. Even though he wasn't the guy to build the Temple (something David wanted very much to do for God), he still was driven to serve the Lord and love the people. In 1 Chronicles, chapter 29, it records that, near the end of his life David was tenaciously exhorting Solomon to be wise and to be faithful to God. David also produced the architectural plans for the Temple, and poured a boat-load of his personal wealth into building it. What made this king, warrior, shepherd and poet driven to follow God, even in his old age? It was his daily practice to always seek God out for forgiveness, healing and wisdom that continually renewed his mind for the Lord.

David's passion to honor God was so great, his mind clear of any MVs, that he left a legacy cherished by Jews and Gentiles. David is seen as Israel's greatest king and his name was and is remembered long after his years on the earth. His star is on Israel's national flag. His exploits are touted in prose and art, and his military prowess studied by soldiers. Yet, what he is most remembered for is what we all want to be—David was *a man after God's own heart.*

WHAT'S YOUR LEGACY?

Stop the mind viruses; plant the good thoughts. Enough good thoughts make a good attitude, a positive attitude builds good habits, good habits drive a destiny, and a good destiny always leaves an eternal legacy. Are you God's pipeline of living water to a thirsty group of coworkers? Are you His roaring stream of clean water that heals a community of people? Are you a wellspring of water for your family and friends? When MVs are driven out, you'll find the strength to go the second mile with people—that supernatural strength—and watch what happens next.

Maybe you'll find yourself eagerly helping someone on the road who has a flat tire. Maybe it's paying for the flowers of someone who wants to honor their deceased loved one. Maybe it is as simple as picking up the check at restaurant for a neighbor. Watch what happens. Watch how the MVs recoil from good works done in Christ's name. Expelling the MVs is the first step to living an abundant life that speaks across time to many generations. Paul said it best, "Therefore, as we have opportunity, let us do good to all people, especially to those who belong to the family of believers" (Galatians 6:10).

All our actions are born from a MV or a good thought—and those actions shape the world around us. Let God fill your mind with thoughts that take you to new heights. Dream big; walk humbly. Imagine good and wonderful things and share those dreams with God in prayer. If you stumble, get up, stay the course, keeping walking for Jesus. Remember you are being transformed from within. If you are willing to listen to the Holy Spirit, meditate on His Word, invite wise people into your life, and dwell on what is noble and praiseworthy, you will shine brightly and effectively resist mind viruses. People will gravitate to you. You will be God's supernatural pump of living water. For the world is thirsty and in great need of His healing waters.

FURTHER DIAGNOSIS

1. Recall a time where you and others were working together for the common good in Christ (a synchro-destiny moment).

2. What caused it? What did you learn?

3. Have you ever seen a widespread change in a community or workplace values or behavior because of the supernatural witness of one or a few people?

4. Have you ever buried a God-given gift, treasure or blessing?

5. What qualities or actions are people thirsty to see in a Christian's daily life?

6. What legacy in God would you like to leave to your family and friends?

7. What would you like to leave for the city or community you live in?

FILLING YOUR PRESCRIPTION

1. A stronghold is a _____ of thoughts.

2. Synchronized diving is a beautiful metaphor for out lives as we _____ with others and the Holy Spirit.

3. Mark Twain, "The two most important days of your life are the day you were born and the day you figure out _____."

4. To achieve our _____ - _____ dreams, we need each other.

5. Dr. Kermit Bridges observed that young people between the ages of 16 and 26 are in the decade of decision. We make three major decisions that influence the direction and course of our lives:

*   Will you make _____ _____ your Lord?
*   What _____ will you choose?
*   Whom will you _____ if you choose to get married?

6. Defeating mind viruses is not only a victory for _____.

7. As God daily transforms our minds from the inside, then the _____ we use will also change.

8. When Jesus comes into a person's life, the old nature doesn't suddenly _____.

9. MVs affect more than our mind – it corrupts relationship, families, communities and even a _____.

10. _____ the MVs is the first step to living abundant life that speaks across time to many generations.

USING THIS BOOK
IN CLASSES AND GROUPS

THIS BOOK IS DESIGNED for individual study, small groups, and classes. The best way to absorb and apply these principles is for each person to individually study and answer the questions at the end of each chapter, and then to discuss them in either a class or a group environment.

Each chapter's questions are designed to promote reflection, application, and discussion. Order enough copies of the book for everyone to have a copy. For couples, encourage both to have their own book so they can record their individual reflections.

A recommended schedule for a small group or class might be:

Week 1: Introduce the material. As a group leader, tell your story, share your hopes for the group, and provide books for each person. Encourage people to read the assigned chapter each week and answer the questions.

Weeks 2–10: Each week, introduce the topic for the week and share a story of how God has used the principles in your life. In small groups, lead people through a discussion of the questions at the end of the chapter. In classes, teach the principles in each chapter, use personal illustrations, and invite discussion.

PERSONALIZE EACH LESSON

Don't feel pressured to cover every question in your group discussions. Pick out three or four that had the biggest impact on you, and focus on those, or ask people in the group to share their responses to the questions that meant the most to them that week.

- Make sure you personalize the principles and applications. At least once in each group meeting, add your own story to illustrate a particular point.

- Make the Scriptures come alive. Far too often, we read the Bible like it's a phone book, with little or no emotion. Paint a vivid picture for people. Provide insights about the context of people's encounters with God, and help people in your class or group sense the emotions of specific people in each scene.

FOCUS ON APPLICATION

The questions at the end of each chapter and your encouragement to group members to be authentic will help your group take big steps to apply the principles they're learning. Share how you are applying the principles in particular chapters each week, and encourage them to take steps of growth, too.

THREE TYPES OF QUESTIONS

If you have led groups for a few years, you already understand the importance of using open questions to stimulate discussion. Three types of questions are *limiting, leading,* and *open.* Many of the questions at the end of each day's lesson are open questions.

Limiting questions focus on an obvious answer, such as, "What does Jesus call Himself in John 10:11?" These don't stimulate reflection or discussion. If you want to use questions like this, follow them with thought-provoking, open questions.

Leading questions require the listener to guess what the leader has in mind, such as, "Why did Jesus use the metaphor of a shepherd in John 10?" (He was probably alluding to a passage in Ezekiel, but many people don't know that). The teacher who asks a leading question has a definite answer in mind. Instead of asking this kind of question, you should just teach the point and perhaps ask an open question about the point you have made.

Open questions usually don't have right or wrong answers. They stimulate thinking, and they are far less threatening because the person answering doesn't risk ridicule for being wrong. These questions often begin with "Why do you think?" or "What are some reasons that?" or "How would you have felt in that situation?"

PREPARATION

As you prepare to teach this material in a group or class, consider these steps:

1. Carefully and thoughtfully read the book. Make notes, highlight key sections, quotes, or stories, and complete the reflection section

at the end of each day's chapter. This will familiarize you with the entire scope of the content.

2. As you prepare for each week's class or group, read the corresponding chapter again and make additional notes.

3. Tailor the amount of content to the time allotted. You won't have time to cover all the questions, so pick the ones that are most pertinent.

4. Add your own stories to personalize the message and add impact.

5. Before and during your preparation, ask God to give you wisdom, clarity, and power. Trust Him to use your group to change people's lives.

6. Most people will get far more out of the group if they read the chapter and complete the reflection each week. Order books before the group or class begins or after the first week.

"FILLING YOUR PRESCRIPTION" ANSWER KEY

CHAPTER 1

1. obeying, straying
2. dormant
3. destructive
4. truth
5. dealing
6. balcony, basement
7. distort, poison
8. conscious
9. moment you awake
10. refuse, negative

CHAPTER 2

1. recognize, biblical
2. assignment
3. appear
4. senses
5. raging
6. sin
7. self-destruction
8. Negative Town
9. spread
10. thoughts

CHAPTER 3

1. spiritual dead
2. religious
3. suffocates
4. stuck
5. head
6. As one thinks, so shall they be
7. successful, failure
8. season
9. maximize
10. decaying

CHAPTER 4

1. breaker box
2. powerful
3. risk
4. faith
5. shake the tree
6. practical
7. deposits, withdrawals
8. at the door
9. Word of God
10. higher thinkers, retrain

CHAPTER 5

1. learned
2. destroy, lifestyle
3. invade, infest
4. borrowed
5. today
6. hatchery.
7. paralyze, petrify

8. performance

9. hungry

10. non-negotiable, preference

CHAPTER 6

1. flourish

2. Despair

3. rewards

4. defense

5. he came to his senses

6. mentally

7. available

8. Detachment

9. perceptions, revealed

10. voice

CHAPTER 7

1. Environment

2. alone, faith

3. raised, influenced

4. courage

5. internet

6. sensed

7. experience

8. regular

9. optimism

10. judge, pray

CHAPTER 8

1. significant limitations

2. lockbox

3. material, spiritual

4. sixth

5. limited

6. commonplace

7. even more

8. train

9. waste management

10. It is written

CHAPTER 9

1. children

2. God's, own

3. line up, honor, help

4. pleasure

5. history

6. knowledge, imagination

7. Do Not Disturb

8. pollute

9. expense

10. choice

11. new

CHAPTER 10

1. household

2. partner

3. why

4. God-inspired

5. Jesus Christ, career, marry

6. yourself

7. words

8. evaporate

9. nation

10. expelling

ABOUT THE AUTHOR

MIKE D. ROBERTSON

What started out with rough beginnings has blossomed into a full time ministry. Some thought he would go the way of the world but Jesus Christ stepped in when he was nineteen. Mike often quips: "I owe everything to  the church. It has given me my friends, a great wife and a purpose for taking up space on the planet."

Mike earned his Bachelor's Degree from Southwestern Assemblies of God University. He went on to earn his Master's of Divinity from Southwestern Baptist Theological Seminary. He pursued his doctoral studies at Fuller Theological Seminary.

The Robertson's were the pastors of Praise Temple, a church in Burleson, Texas when they received a "God Nudge" to go to Southern California. It was in Oceanside that they planted Family Fellowship Church, and were the pastors there for fifteen years.

Mike then became the Vice President of University Advancement at Southwestern Assemblies of God University (SAGU) in Waxahachie, Texas. In 2008, Mike and Karen became the Lead Pastors of Visalia First Assembly in Visalia, CA.

RESOURCES

The God Nudge

One of the greatest privileges of our lives is for the God of the universe to share His heart with us. If we'll learn to listen, He'll prompt us to be involved in His work of touching lives. In this book, Pastor Mike Robertson explains the wonders and the warnings of being nudged by God. Pay attention. The concepts, stories, and applications will revolutionize your relationship with God.

I Shook Hands with Death

What happens when we die? This question has haunted people since time began. Mike Robertson's near-death experience enabled him to find a clear, comforting answer. When he faced death, he became convinced that he no longer had anything to fear. He had put his life in Jesus' hands, and Jesus would welcome him home.

I Be Jokin'...

The number one problem with public speakers today is that the attention span of the audience has been shortened. Today's culture has been so inundated with sitcoms and nine-minute content segments that after about ten minutes, you have lost them. I think that every 30-minute speech ought to have at least half a dozen points that will make people laugh. Humor endears the audience to the speaker and they become more receptive to what the speaker is saying.

For more information about these and other resources, go to:

www.mikedrobertson.com

Follow Mike on:

Twitter: @pastormikedrob
Instagram: pastormikedrob

NOTES:

NOTES:

NOTES:

NOTES: